house beautiful®
THE DESIGNS OF
WILLIAM E. POOLE

Design Q140, page 94

70 CLASSICAL HOUSE PLANS
In The Southern Tradition

HOME PLANNERS
TUCSON, ARIZONA

Published by Home Planners, LLC
Wholly owned by Hanley-Wood, LLC
Editorial and Corporate Offices:
3275 West Ina Road, Suite 110
Tucson, Arizona 85741

Distribution Center:
29333 Lorie Lane
Wixom, Michigan 48393

Rickard D. Bailey, CEO and Publisher
Cindy Coatsworth Lewis, Director of Publishing
Jan Prideaux, Executive Editor
Paul Fitzgerald, Senior Designer

Photo Credit
Front Cover: Freda Wilkins

First Printing, September, 1997

10 9 8 7 6 5 4 3

Printed in the United States of America

Library of Congress Catalog Card Number: 97-73706
ISBN softcover: 1-881955-40-0

House Beautiful is a registered trademark of The Hearst Corporation.

Table of Contents

These picturesque cottages create special getaways that keep the romance of the South alive, representing well-established design from the East Coast to the West, and from the deep South through New England.

Combining the formality and polish of classical styling with the charm that envelops a home in warmth, these homes truly represent the renowned hospitality of the South. Captivating entrances provide a fine introduction into interiors that capture the magic of true hometown hospitality.

Designed to embody the essence of early Southern-style tradition, these homes inspire those interested in making new histories. Gothic columns and favorite "All-American" building attributes such as the use of brick, wood siding and dormer windows enhance the rich, traditional appeal of these plans.

The large proportions and embellishments such as grand columns that help define the style of these designs make a lasting impression. The splendor of these homes—graced with contemporary floor plans—are filled with amenities that embellish the art of living well.

It is with great pride and pleasure that I introduce the home plans of noted residential designer William E. Poole. A true Southerner and a romantic at heart, a believer in the proper balance and proportions of classical design, his homes have a distinctive flavor all their own. With strict attention to details, function, form and a love of architectural "rightness", William's singular purpose is to create homes that reflect the beauty and grace of timeless design. I encourage you to make the place where you live the place that you love . . .

Annette Stramesi
Editor
Colonial Homes

Editor's Note

Williffiam E. Poole is a man of extraordinary talent. From an early age, he had a passion for design. Though his inspiration clearly comes from the region he knows and loves—the South—his vision transcends regionality and extends to any part of the country one chooses to call "home." Perhaps the brightest facet of Mr. Poole's design skill is his remarkable ability to accommodate a comfort zone—filling each home with amenities tailored to fit the owner's personal lifestyle.

As each chapter in America's architecture closes, another opens. Each new episode develops its own story like a well-written novel—unfolding with a glance at the past, a focus on the present and an eye toward the future. It is this evolution of design that becomes a part of our heritage. William Poole's collection of All-American styles successfully combines the architectural integrity of the past with thoughtfully-planned interiors and the luxurious details of today—making each home a true contemporary classic.

As you study the plans in the chapters that follow, you will find none of the sameness that is so pervasive in many of today's designs. Browsing through the collection, you will soon discover that the picturesque designs of Mr. Poole are equally at home tucked into big-city neighborhoods, nestled behind picket fences, or along small-town streets. From grand homes with elaborate verandas and porticos to cottages embellished with colorful shutters and chimneys that hint of cozy hearths within—one thing is certain, each design is a creation that will capture the spirit of your imagination and help define in your mind the place called "home."

Romantic Cottages and Getaways

*I*f it's a utopian getaway you desire, Romantic Cottages and Getaways contains homes that provide romance in epic proportions. With inspiration drawn from such wondrous places as the West Indies—and from Carmel's craggy coastline to the pristine countryside of Connecticut—there is something for everyone. These plans extend an invitation to enjoy your home as you enjoy your life—to the fullest.

Delicate patterns of lace and gingerbread trim have been connected to the definitive style of Victoriana since its romantic beginnings. The Cape May (page 10) rekindles the charm of that golden era, and invites you to share in the delight of those simpler, gentler times.

Perhaps you long to relax amid the gently rolling hills and lush green landscape of the European countryside. The Carmel Cottage (page 18) can help you recreate that feeling in many different countryside settings. The charming outdoor dining terrace with its foliage-covered trellis, will help you take full advantage of nature's generosity while bringing the experience, the magic, of Old-World ambiance to your door.

Or you may opt to sit in companionable silence, stretched out in Adirondack chairs with a cool drink on a warm evening, watching as the last remnant of sunlight sets behind your cozy country home. It doesn't ever get better than that! Take a look at the aptly named Adirondack (page 31), and you will see exactly what we mean.

Variety, the spice of life, places its mark on each cottage in this chapter—filling them with the delightful charm that makes them truly romantic getaways.

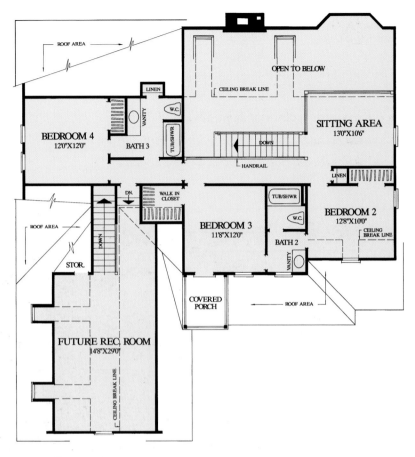

Upper Level Floor Plan labels:

ROOF AREA

BEDROOM 4
12'0"X12'0"

LINEN

VANITY

W.C.

BATH 3

TUB/SHWR

OPEN TO BELOW

CEILING BREAK LINE

SITTING AREA
13'0"X10'6"

DOWN

HANDRAIL

LINEN

DN.

WALK IN CLOSET

TUB/SHWR

W.C.

BEDROOM 2
12'8"X10'0"

CEILING BREAK LINE

ROOF AREA

UP

STOR.

BEDROOM 3
11'8"X12'0"

BATH 2

VANITY

COVERED PORCH

ROOF AREA

FUTURE REC. ROOM
14'8"X29'0"

CEILING BREAK LINE

Info box:

Main Level: 1,809 square feet
Upper Level: 944 square feet
Total: 2,753 square feet
Future Recreation Room:
  440 square feet
Optional basement plan is included

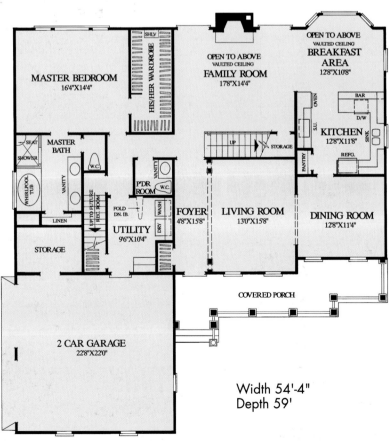

Main Level Floor Plan labels:

SHLV

MASTER BEDROOM
16'4"X14'4"

HIS/HER WARDROBE

OPEN TO ABOVE
VAULTED CEILING
FAMILY ROOM
17'8"X14'4"

OPEN TO ABOVE
VAULTED CEILING
BREAKFAST AREA
12'8"X10'8"

BAR

D/W

S.U. OVEN

SEAT

SHOWER

MASTER BATH

VANITY

W.C.

WHIRLPOOL TUB

VANITY

LINEN

UP

STORAGE

KITCHEN
12'8"X11'8"

PANTRY

SINK

REFG.

FOLD DN. lB.

UP TO FUTURE REC. ROOM

PDR ROOM

VANITY

W.C.

WASH

DRY

UTILITY
9'6"X10'4"

STORAGE

FOYER
4'8"X15'8"

LIVING ROOM
13'0"X15'8"

DINING ROOM
12'8"X11'4"

COVERED PORCH

2 CAR GARAGE
22'8"X22'0"

Width 54'-4"
Depth 59'

Cape May—Design Q100

What a charming town! All along the streets sit cottages of exquisite detail—which one shall it be? Which one will shelter us in storms and hold us tenderly throughout our summer days? This is it, Cape May, our home of choice. None other could match its warmth, its intricate design, its romantic charm.

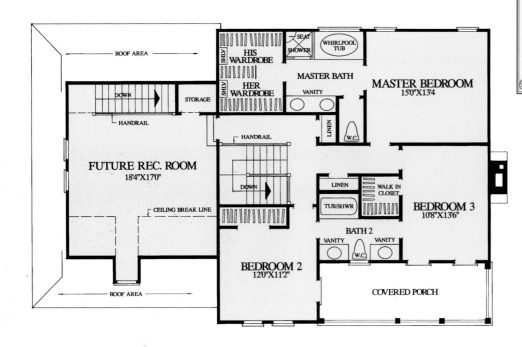

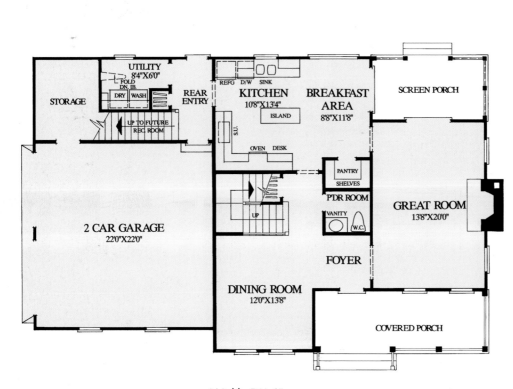

Main Level: 1,075 square feet
Upper Level: 994 square feet
Total: 2,069 square feet
Future Recreation Room:
  382 square feet
Optional basement plan is included

ROOF AREA

HIS WARDROBE

SHLV

SEAT SHOWER

WHIRLPOOL TUB

MASTER BATH

MASTER BEDROOM
15'0"X13'4"

DOWN

HANDRAIL

STORAGE

SHLV

HER WARDROBE

VANITY

LINEN

W.C.

HANDRAIL

FUTURE REC. ROOM
18'4"X170"

DOWN

LINEN

WALK IN CLOSET

BEDROOM 3
10'8"X13'6"

CEILING BREAK LINE

TUB/SHWR

VANITY

W.C.

VANITY

BATH 2

BEDROOM 2
12'0"X11'2"

COVERED PORCH

ROOF AREA

UTILITY
8'4"X6'0"

FOLD DN. IB.

REFG   D/W   SINK

SCREEN PORCH

STORAGE

DRY   WASH

REAR ENTRY

KITCHEN
10'8"X13'4"

ISLAND

BREAKFAST AREA
8'8"X11'8"

UP TO FUTURE REC. ROOM

STU.

OVEN   DESK

PANTRY

SHELVES

2 CAR GARAGE
22'0"X22'0"

UP

PDR ROOM

VANITY

W.C.

GREAT ROOM
13'8"X20'0"

FOYER

DINING ROOM
12'0"X13'8"

COVERED PORCH

Width 56'-4"
Depth 35'-4"

West Indies Cottage—Design Q101

Blue waters of the Caribbean wash lazily over colorful seashells that decorate white, pink and black sandy beaches. Bright colors of the rainbow attach themselves to the cluster of cottages lining the shore. Laughter trickles outward from the palm-strewn beaches. The musical beat of the islands rises to meet us as we arrive at the West Indies Cottage—our romantic hideaway.

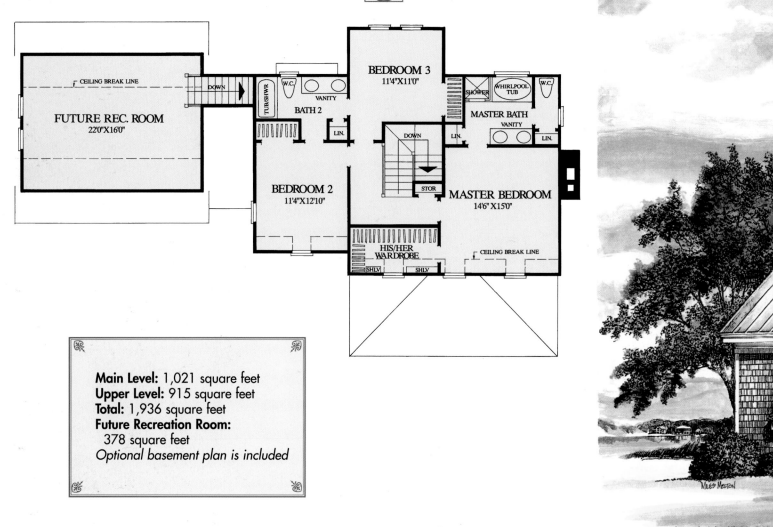

FUTURE REC. ROOM
22'0"X16'0"

CEILING BREAK LINE

DOWN

TUB/SHWR

W.C.

VANITY

BATH 2

LIN.

BEDROOM 3
11'4"X11'0"

SHOWER

WHIRLPOOL TUB

W.C.

MASTER BATH

VANITY

LIN.

LIN.

DOWN

STOR.

MASTER BEDROOM
14'6" X 15'0"

BEDROOM 2
11'4"X12'10"

HIS/HER WARDROBE

SHLV

SHLV

CEILING BREAK LINE

Main Level: 1,021 square feet
Upper Level: 915 square feet
Total: 1,936 square feet
Future Recreation Room:
 378 square feet
Optional basement plan is included

2 CAR GARAGE
22'0"X22'0"

UP TO FUTURE REC ROOM

WINDOW SEAT

DINING ROOM
11'4"X11'0"

WASH   DRY

BREAKFAST AREA
11'4"X10'0"

PANTRY

UP

STOR.

GREAT ROOM
14'0"X23'4"

PORCH

REFG.

ISLAND   BAR

RANGE

KITCHEN
11'4"X10'8"

D/W   SINK

SINK

PDR RM.

W.C.

FOYER

Width 66'-8"
Depth 38'-8"

PORCH

Ocracoke Cottage—Design Q102

A little cottage on a small island off the coast of North Carolina harkens back to the earliest of times. Many a yarn has been spun about pirates, fair maidens and such; but, the truth of the matter is that families held together the fabric of Ocracoke Island then as they do now—gathering at dusk in their own Ocracoke Cottage.

Telluride—Design Q103

Rugged mountain peaks, lush green valleys, wide open spaces...this is Telluride. A charming Victorian village filled with delightful cottages on picturesque streets, rodeos beneath blazing blue skies, cherry cokes at the corner store and moms pushing baby carriages. Life goes on in Telluride—where your home is certain to enhance your lifestyle.

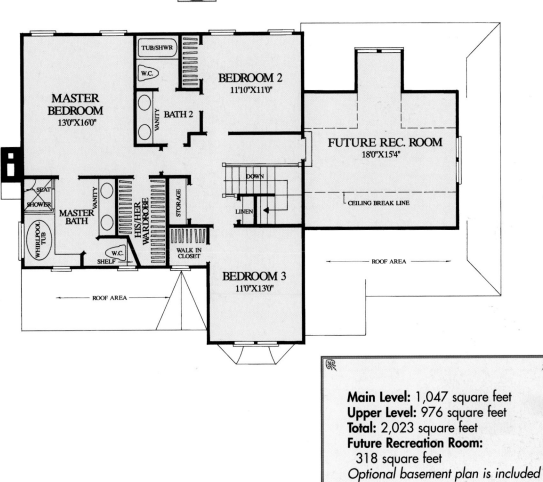

Upper Level

MASTER BEDROOM 13'0"X16'0"

TUB/SHWR
W.C.
VANITY
BATH 2

BEDROOM 2 11'10"X11'0"

FUTURE REC. ROOM 18'0"X15'4"

CEILING BREAK LINE

SEAT
SHOWER
MASTER BATH
WHIRLPOOL TUB
VANITY
W.C.
SHELF
HIS/HER WARDROBE
STORAGE
WALK IN CLOSET

DOWN
LINEN

ROOF AREA

BEDROOM 3 11'0"X13'0"

ROOF AREA

Main Level: 1,047 square feet
Upper Level: 976 square feet
Total: 2,023 square feet
Future Recreation Room:
  318 square feet
Optional basement plan is included

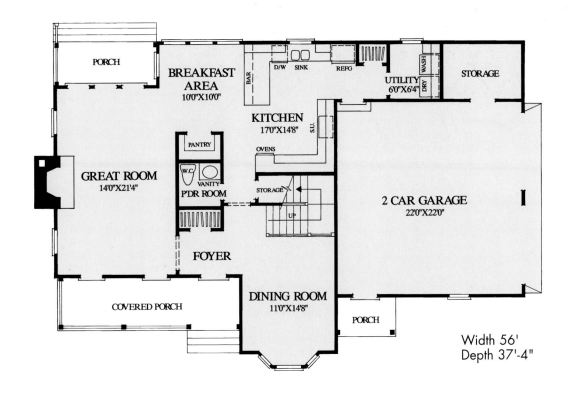

PORCH

BREAKFAST AREA 10'0"X10'0"

BAR
D/W
SINK
REFG

UTILITY 6'0"X6'4"
WASH
DRY
STORAGE

KITCHEN 17'0"X14'8"
S.U.

GREAT ROOM 14'0"X21'4"

PANTRY
W.C
VANITY
P'DR ROOM

OVENS

STORAGE
UP

2 CAR GARAGE 22'0"X22'0"

FOYER

COVERED PORCH

DINING ROOM 11'0"X14'8"

PORCH

Width 56'
Depth 37'-4"

Upper Level

ROOF AREA

ROOF AREA

STORAGE

OPEN TO BELOW

CEILING BREAK LINE

BEDROOM 4
12'0"X10'0"

BEDROOM 2
14'0"X15'0"

TUB/SHWR

W.C.

BATH 2

VANITY

CEILING BREAK LINE

HANDRAIL

TUB/SHWR

W.C.

BALCONY

BATH 3

VANITY

STORAGE

LINEN

LIN

OPEN TO BELOW

DWN

FUTURE REC. ROOM
21'8"X23'0"

BEDROOM 3
13'2"X12'8"

CEILING BREAK LINE

CEILING BREAK LINE

ROOF AREA

Main Level: 1,805 square feet
Upper Level: 952 square feet
Total: 2,757 square feet
Future Recreation Room:
   475 square feet
Optional basement plan is included

BREAKFAST AREA
11'4"X8'8"

PANTRY

ENTERTAINMENT CENTER

OPEN TO ABOVE

VAULTED CEILING
FAMILY ROOM
17'8"X18'0"

BAR

D.W.

SINK

ISLAND

RANGE OVENS

KITCHEN
12'4"X12'4"

REFG.

MASTER BEDROOM
17'0"X13'0"

STOR

WOOD TRELLIS

SHOWER

VANITY

LINEN

DINING ROOM
12'0"X12'8"

DINING TERRACE

WHIRLPOOL TUB

MASTER BATH

WASH

DRY

VANITY

PDR ROOM

STUCCO WALL

W.C.

HIS/HER WARDROBE

UTILITY
7'6"X8'0"

W.C.

LIN

UP

VAULTED CEILING
FOYER
9'4"X14'8"

LIVING ROOM
15'4"X13'8"

2 CAR GARAGE
21'8"X23'0"

PORCH

STORAGE

Width 48'-10"
Depth 64'-10"

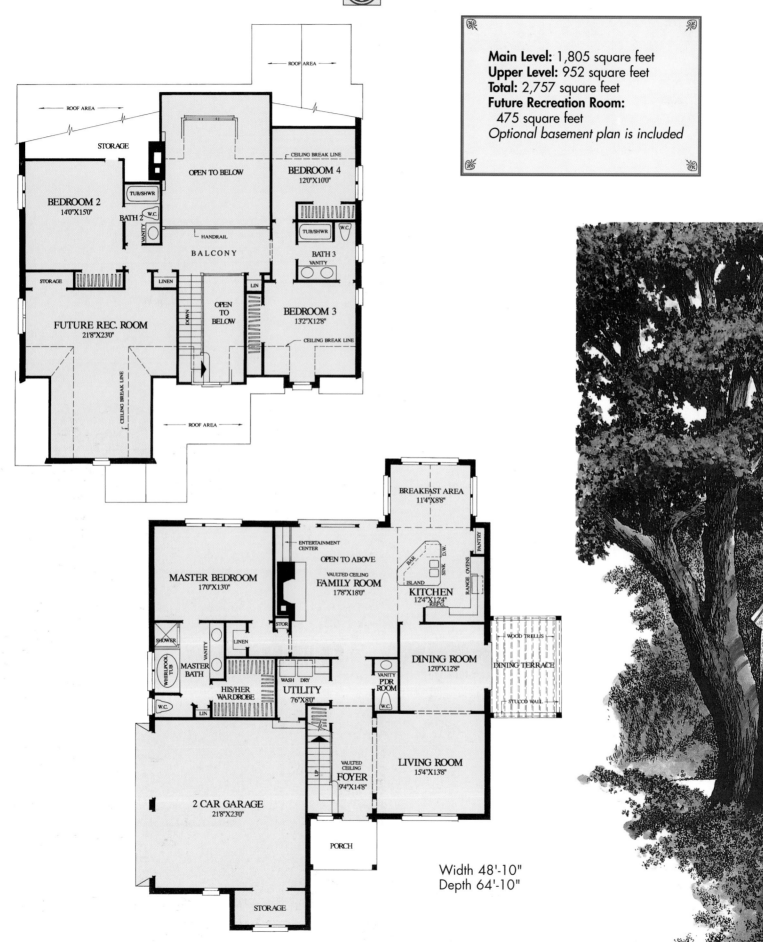

Carmel Cottage—Design Q104

*T*he winding streets, the quaint little shops, the pounding surf, the tree-covered land—the setting for Carmel Cottage. Warm, weathered and welcoming, this home endures the test of time and embraces all who pause to admire.

Myers Park—Design Q105

The answer to your imagination's vision—an old neighborhood right in the center of things—good schools, lush plantings and large, old trees. A solid home that appears to have stories to tell; a porch where family and friends gather; shady, tree-lined sidewalks up and down the street—Myers Park, always "home".

Main Level: 1,305 square feet
Upper Level: 1,052 square feet
Total: 2,357 square feet
Future Recreation Room:
    430 square feet
Optional Basement:
    1,305 square feet

ROOF AREA

ROOF AREA

DOWN

CEILING BREAK LINE

FUTURE REC. ROOM
27'4"X14'0"

ROOF AREA

BEDROOM 2
12'0"X11'0"

TUB/SHWR

W.C.

LINEN

VAN

BATH 2

HIS WARDROBE

HER WARDROBE

MASTER BEDROOM
13'0"X16'0"

BALCONY
HANDRAIL

DOWN

VAN

VAN

VAN

LIN

BEDROOM 3
13'0"X 12'2"

OPEN TO BELOW

MASTER BATH

SHWR

SEAT

WHIRLPOOL TUB

W.C.

CATHEDRAL CEILING
BREAKFAST AREA
10'4"X11'0"

UP TO FUTURE
REC ROOM

FAMILY ROOM
15'2"X18'0"

ISLAND
BAR
SINK D/W

KITCHEN
12'10"X11'4"

RANGE

REFRG

DINING ROOM
13'0"X11'4"

STOR

ENTERTAINMENT CENTER

PANTRY

UP

2 CAR GARAGE
22'0"X24'0"

UTILITY
9'4"X8'8"

WASH DRY

SINK

P'DR RM

VAN

W.C.

TWO STORY CEILING
FOYER
10'2"X8'8"

LIVING ROOM
13'0"X15'0"

PORCH

Width 69'-4"
Depth 35'-10"

Main Level: 1,498 square feet
Upper Level: 1,450 square feet
Total: 2,948 square feet
Future Recreation Room:
  423 square feet
Optional basement plan is included

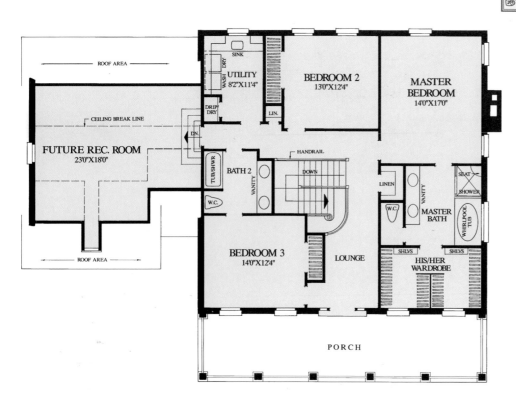

ROOF AREA

CEILING BREAK LINE

FUTURE REC. ROOM
23'0"X18'0"

ROOF AREA

SINK

WASH DRY

UTILITY
8'2"X11'4"

DRIP DRY

LIN.

TUB/SHWR

BATH 2

VANITY

BEDROOM 2
13'0"X12'4"

LIN.

HANDRAIL

DOWN

W.C.

BEDROOM 3
14'0"X12'4"

LOUNGE

LINEN

W.C.

VANITY

MASTER BEDROOM
14'0"X17'0"

SEAT

SHOWER

WHIRLPOOL TUB

MASTER BATH

SHLVS

SHLVS

HIS/HER WARDROBE

PORCH

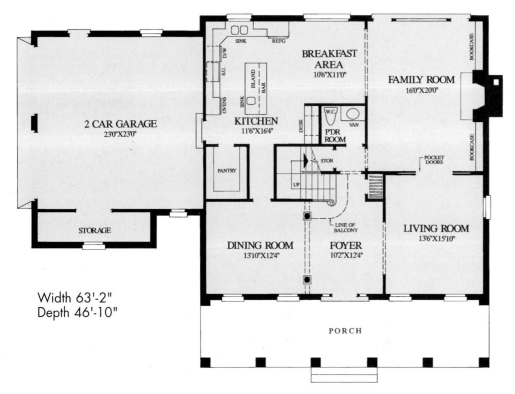

2 CAR GARAGE
23'0"X23'0"

STORAGE

SINK

REFG

D/W

S.U.

OVENS

SINK

ISLAND

BAR

KITCHEN
11'6"X16'4"

PANTRY

DESK

W.C.

VAN

P'DR ROOM

STOR

UP

BREAKFAST AREA
10'6"X11'0"

BOOKCASE

FAMILY ROOM
16'0"X20'0"

POCKET DOORS

BOOKCASE

LINE OF BALCONY

DINING ROOM
13'10"X12'4"

FOYER
10'2"X12'4"

LIVING ROOM
13'6"X15'10"

PORCH

Width 63'-2"
Depth 46'-10"

Beaumont—Design Q106

Wisteria vines wind 'round the huge trunk of the old live oak. Butterflies flit amid the buttercups, birds chirp to greet the morn and all awaken to the sweet smell of honeysuckle. The Beaumont stirs with these awakenings and busies itself preparing for another day.

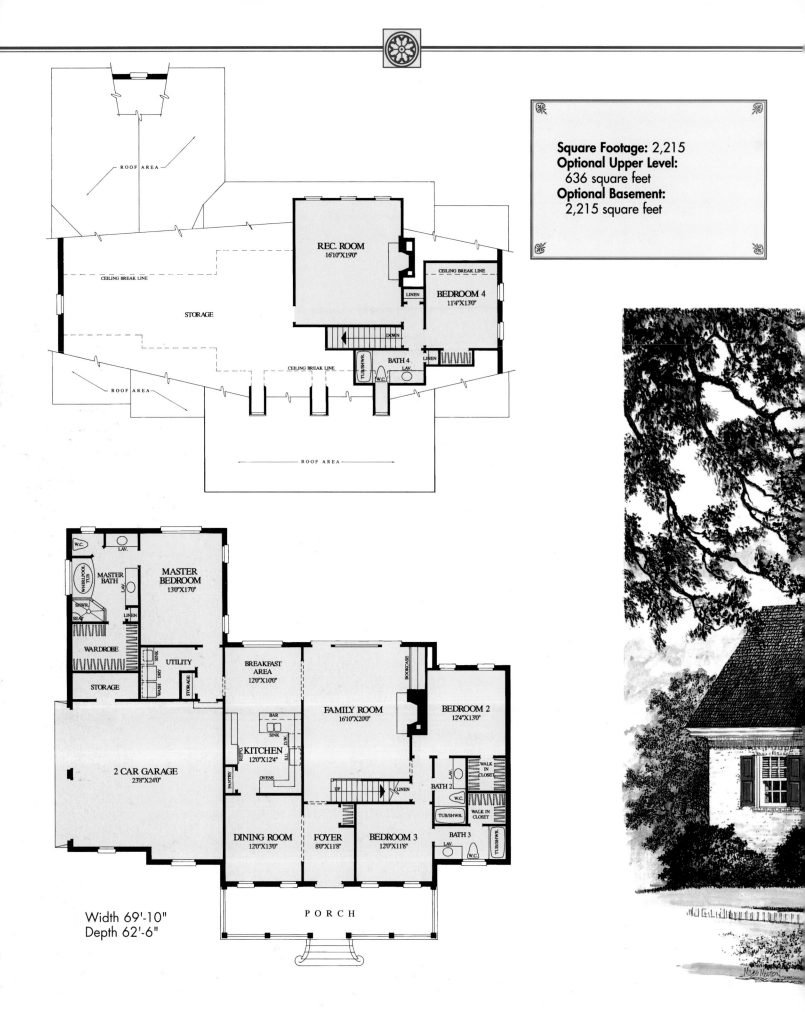

ROOF AREA

REC. ROOM
16'0"X19'0"

CEILING BREAK LINE

CEILING BREAK LINE

BEDROOM 4
11'4"X13'0"

LINEN

STORAGE

DOWN

CEILING BREAK LINE

LINEN

BATH 4

TUB/SHWR.

LAV.

W.C.

ROOF AREA

ROOF AREA

Square Footage: 2,215
Optional Upper Level:
636 square feet
Optional Basement:
2,215 square feet

W.C.

LAV.

WHIRLPOOL TUB

MASTER
BATH

LAV.

MASTER
BEDROOM
13'0"X17'0"

SHWR.

SEAT

LINEN

WARDROBE

SINK

UTILITY

STORAGE

WASH

DRY

STORAGE

BREAKFAST
AREA
12'0"X10'0"

BAR

SINK

FAMILY ROOM
16'10"X20'0"

BOOKCASE

BEDROOM 2
12'4"X13'0"

2 CAR GARAGE
23'8"X24'0"

REFRIG.

KITCHEN
12'0"X12'4"

D.W.

S.U.

PANTRY

OVENS

UP

LINEN

BATH 2

LAV.

WALK IN
CLOSET

W.C.

TUB/SHWR.

WALK IN
CLOSET

Width 69'-10"
Depth 62'-6"

DINING ROOM
12'0"X13'0"

FOYER
8'0"X11'8"

BEDROOM 3
12'0"X11'8"

BATH 3

LAV.

W.C.

TUB/SHWR.

PORCH

Chevy Chase—Design Q107

*A*dministrations change. History is made. Policies are set. Technology advances. The pace is fast—the future unknown. The result: stress. Yet solace—that elusive element in our lives, is found each day in the circle of friends and family, in the space of home—at Chevy Chase.

Virginia Farmhouse—Design Q108

It has been said that there is a reason for all things and that for all things there is a season. The original farmhouses were of local materials and well-balanced. The porches provided shade and shelter, the dormers provided light in the upper half-story and the season for this Virginia Farmhouse is—forevermore.

ROOF AREA

ROOF AREA

OPEN TO BELOW

WHIRLPOOL TUB

W.C.

BATH 2

BEDROOM 2
11'9"X13'4"

STORAGE

LINEN

HANDRAIL

BALCONY

LAUNDRY CHUTE

VAN.

DOWN

DOWN

BATH 3

TUB/SHWR.

W.C.

VAN.

BEDROOM 4
13'4"X13'5"

DOWN

OPEN TO BELOW

BEDROOM 3
14'4"X13'5"

CEILING BREAK LINE

FUTURE REC. ROOM
17'4"X21'0"

CEILING BREAK LINE

ROOF AREA

MASTER BEDROOM
17'4"X13'4"

SCREEN PORCH

SEAT

W.C.

SHWR

WARDROBE

KITCHEN
10'2"X13'4"

D.W. SINK

BREAKFAST AREA
9'6"X15'4"
VAULTED CEILING

FAMILY ROOM
20'8"X15'4"

MASTER BATH

WHIRLPOOL TUB

VANITY

LINEN

REFR.

ISLAND

BAR

LINE OF BALCONY

STORAGE

UP TO FUTURE REC. ROOM

FOLD DN. IRONING BD.

DRY WASH

PANTRY

OVENS DESK

PICT. DOORS

P'DR. ROOM

W.C.

VAN.

UTILITY
9'8"X10'3"

SINK

DINING ROOM
13'4"X15'0"

UP

LIVING ROOM
11'4"X15'0"

2 CAR GARAGE
21'4"X23'0"

PORCH

TWO STORY CEL. FOYER
10'10"X13'2"

PORCH

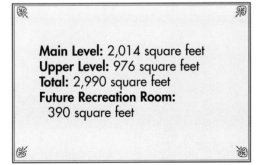
Width 73'-9"
Depth 55'-5"

Carolina Coastal Cottage—Design Q109

Restoration is afoot. Charming cottages being refurbished with loving care abound. However, if the idea of restoration is not your cup of tea, the Carolina Coastal Cottage is designed with you in mind. Built correctly, it will stand the test of time just as well as those that came before it. Enjoy!

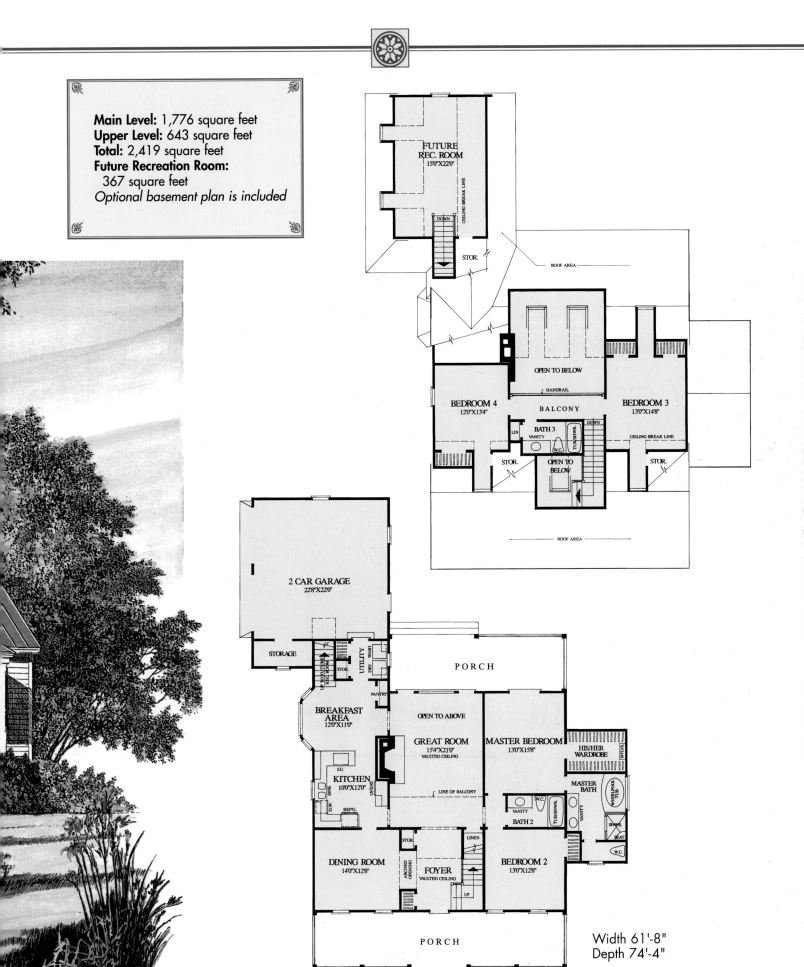

Main Level: 1,776 square feet
Upper Level: 643 square feet
Total: 2,419 square feet
Future Recreation Room:
  367 square feet
Optional basement plan is included

FUTURE REC. ROOM
15'0"X22'0"

CEILING BREAK LINE

DOWN

STOR.

ROOF AREA

OPEN TO BELOW

HANDRAIL

BEDROOM 4
12'0"X13'4"

BALCONY

BEDROOM 3
13'0"X14'8"

LIN

BATH 3

VANITY

W.C.

TUB/SHWR.

DOWN

CEILING BREAK LINE

STOR.

OPEN TO BELOW

STOR.

ROOF AREA

2 CAR GARAGE
22'8"X22'0"

STORAGE

UTILITY

WASH

DRY

PORCH

STOR.

UP TO FUTURE REC. ROOM

BREAKFAST AREA
12'0"X11'0"

PANTRY

OPEN TO ABOVE

MASTER BEDROOM
13'0"X15'8"

HIS/HER WARDROBE

SHLVS.

S.U.

GREAT ROOM
15'4"X21'0"
VAULTED CEILING

MASTER BATH

WHIRLPOOL TUB

KITCHEN
10'0"X12'0"

SINK

OPENS

LINE OF BALCONY

W.C.

VANITY

D.W.

REFG.

VANITY

TUB/SHWR.

BATH 2

SHWR.

SEAT

DINING ROOM
14'0"X12'8"

STOR.

LINEN

BEDROOM 2
13'0"X12'8"

W.C.

ARCHED OPENING

FOYER
VAULTED CEILING

UP

PORCH

Width 61'-8"
Depth 74'-4"

Adirondack—Design Q110

The large old adirondack camps were the inspiration for this exquisite Adirondack Cottage. The sensitive use of twig design is delicately detailed in this lovely home. So right in the mountains, so right in the farmlands, so right in any setting where it can blend with the surrounding beauty of nature itself.

Main Level: 1,712 square feet
Upper Level: 668 square feet
Total: 2,380 square feet
Future Recreation Room:
    573 square feet
Optional Basement:
    1,712 square feet

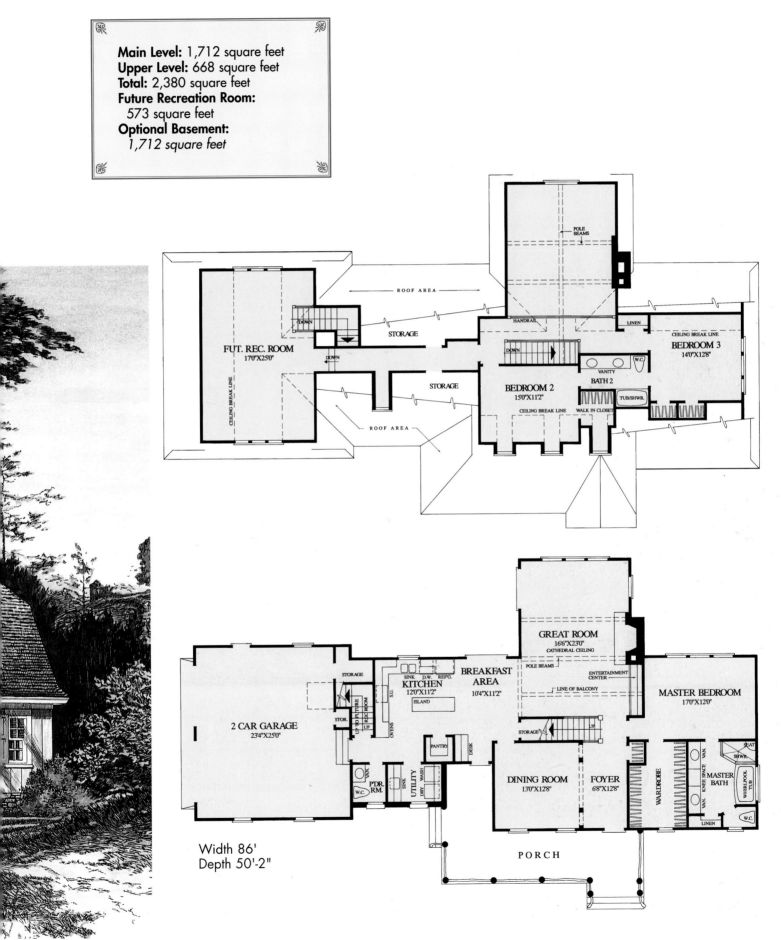

POLE BEAMS

ROOF AREA

DOWN

STORAGE

HANDRAIL

LINEN

CEILING BREAK LINE

BEDROOM 3
14'0"X12'8"

FUT. REC. ROOM
17'0"X25'0"

DOWN

DOWN

W.C.

VANITY

CEILING BREAK LINE

STORAGE

BEDROOM 2
15'0"X11'2"

BATH 2

TUB/SHWR.

CEILING BREAK LINE

WALK IN CLOSET

ROOF AREA

GREAT ROOM
16'6"X23'0"
CATHEDRAL CEILING

STORAGE

SINK   D.W.   REFG.

BREAKFAST
AREA
10'4"X11'2"

POLE BEAMS

ENTERTAINMENT
CENTER

LINE OF BALCONY

MASTER BEDROOM
17'0"X12'0"

KITCHEN
12'0"X11'2"

S.U.

ISLAND

UP TO FUTURE REC ROOM

UP

OVENS

STORAGE

UP

WARDROBE

KNEE SPACE   VAN.

SEAT

SHWR.

VAN.

MASTER
BATH

2 CAR GARAGE
23'4"X25'0"

STOR.

PANTRY

DESK

DINING ROOM
13'0"X12'8"

FOYER
6'8"X12'8"

WHIRLPOOL TUB

VAN.

P'DR.
RM.

W.C.

SINK

UTILITY

DRY   WASH

VAN.

LINEN

W.C.

Width 86'
Depth 50'-2"

PORCH

Planters Cottage — Design Q111

Planters cottages were raised, 1½-story homes that overlooked the rivers and captured their breezes. Though life was hard in those early times, each day began fresh amid the first rays of light and closed with the promise of another peaceful night.

Main Level: 1,556 square feet
Upper Level: 623 square feet
Total: 2,179 square feet
Future Recreation Room:
  368 square feet
Optional basement plan is included

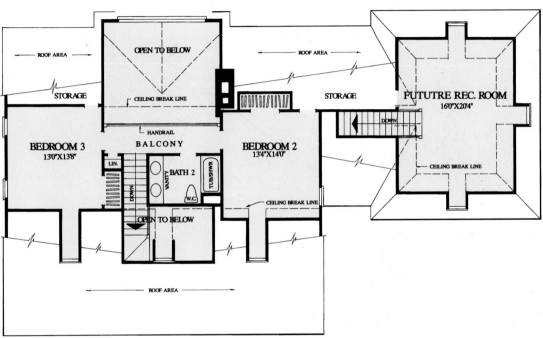

ROOF AREA

OPEN TO BELOW

ROOF AREA

STORAGE

CEILING BREAK LINE

STORAGE

FUTUTRE REC. ROOM
16'0"X20'4"

HANDRAIL

DOWN

BEDROOM 3
13'0"X13'8"

BALCONY

BEDROOM 2
13'4"X14'0"

LIN.

DOWN

VANITY

BATH 2

TUB/SHWR

W.C.

CEILING BREAK LINE

CEILING BREAK LINE

OPEN TO BELOW

ROOF AREA

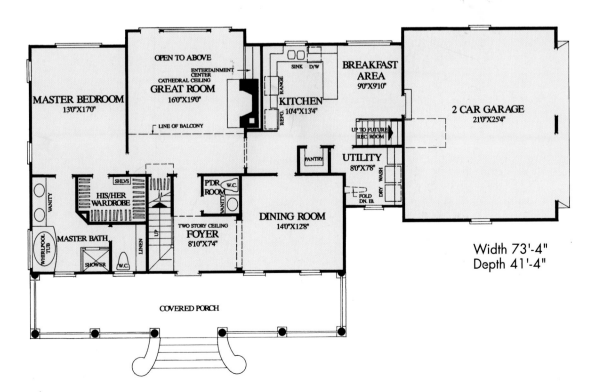

OPEN TO ABOVE

ENTERTAINMENT
CENTER

CATHEDRAL CEILING
GREAT ROOM
16'0"X19'0"

SINK D/W

**BREAKFAST
AREA**
9'0"X9'10"

RANGE

KITCHEN
10'4"X13'4"

REFG.

2 CAR GARAGE
21'0"X25'4"

MASTER BEDROOM
13'0"X17'0"

LINE OF BALCONY

UP TO FUTURE
REC. ROOM

UTILITY
8'0"X7'8"

DRY WASH

SHLVS

HIS/HER
WARDROBE

P'DR
ROOM

W.C.

PANTRY

FOLD
DN. IB.

VANITY

VANITY

TWO STORY CEILING
FOYER
8'10"X7'4"

DINING ROOM
14'0"X12'8"

LINEN

UP

WHIRLPOOL
TUB

MASTER BATH

SHOWER

W.C.

Width 73'-4"
Depth 41'-4"

COVERED PORCH

Connecticut Cottage—Design Q112

*A*n endearing and enduring American original—our Connecticut Cottage. Straight forward and of spare design, yet warm, cozy and uncomplicated...this home snaps things of the past into sharp focus for the pure pleasure of today. The Connecticut Cottage is a home that fits your lifestyle, your very soul.

ROOF AREA

STORAGE

LINEN
W.C.
SHLV

VANITY
BATH 2
TUB/SHWR
WALK IN CLOSET

BEDROOM 2
13'4"X13'0"

DOWN

CEILING BREAK LINE

DOWN

FUTURE REC. ROOM
22'0"X16'0"

ROOF AREA

BEDROOM 3
13'6"X11'8"

CEILING BREAK LINE

OPEN TO BELOW

ROOF AREA

ROOF AREA

Main Level: 1,211 square feet
Upper Level: 551 square feet
Total: 1,762 square feet
Future Recreation Room:
  378 square feet
Optional basement plan is included

MASTER BEDROOM
13'4"X15'0"

GREAT ROOM
21'4"X19'8"

STORAGE

VANITY

HIS/HER WARDROBE

STOR.

DINING AREA

UP TO FUTURE REC. ROOM
STOR.

2 CAR GARAGE
22'0"X22'0"

SHLVS

WHIRLPOOL TUB

MASTER BATH

W.C.

UP

ISLAND

DRY   WASH

REFG.

PRIVACY SHUTTERS
WINDOW SEAT

W.C.

VANITY

TWO STORY CEILING

RANGE

KITCHEN
13'6"X11'8"

SHOWER SEAT

PDR ROOM

FOYER
7'6"X11'4"

D/W   SINK

PORCH

Width 64'-4"
Depth 39'-4"

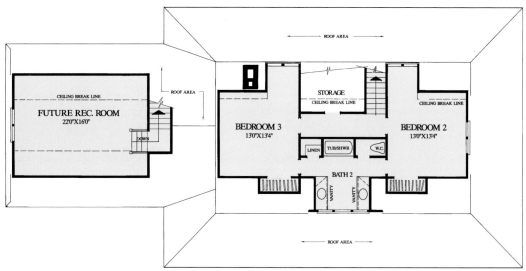

FUTURE REC. ROOM
22'0"X16'0"

CEILING BREAK LINE

ROOF AREA

DOWN

ROOF AREA

STORAGE
CEILING BREAK LINE

BEDROOM 3
13'0"X13'4"

BEDROOM 2
13'0"X13'4"

CEILING BREAK LINE

LINEN

TUB/SHWR

W.C.

BATH 2

VANITY

VANITY

ROOF AREA

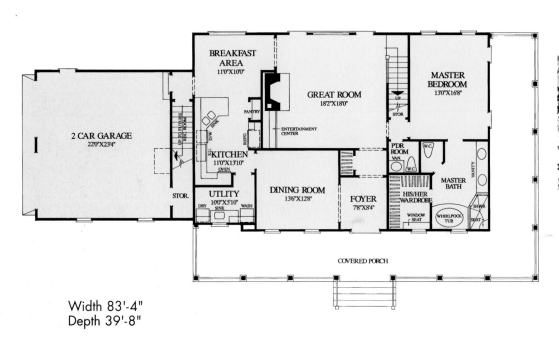

BREAKFAST
AREA
11'0"X10'0"

GREAT ROOM
18'2"X18'0"

MASTER
BEDROOM
13'0"X16'8"

UP.
STOR.

PANTRY

ENTERTAINMENT
CENTER

P'DR
ROOM

W.C.

VAN.

W.C.

MASTER
BATH

VANITY

2 CAR GARAGE
22'0"X23'4"

UP TO FUTURE REC. ROOM

SINK
D/W

KITCHEN
11'0"X13'10"

OVEN

HIS/HER
WARDROBE

STOR.

UTILITY
10'0"X5'10"

DINING ROOM
13'6"X12'8"

FOYER
7'8"X8'4"

WINDOW
SEAT

WHIRLPOOL
TUB

SHWR

SEAT

DRY

SINK

WASH

COVERED PORCH

Width 83'-4"
Depth 39'-8"

Main Level: 1,601 square feet
Upper Level: 667 square feet
Total: 2,268 square feet
Future Recreation Room:
    378 square feet
Optional basement plan is included

Sullivans Island—Design Q113

$\mathcal{A}$ short commute. A lazy holiday. A family gathering place. A rambling porch, gentle breezes, refreshing pink lemonades and evenings under the stars...Sullivans Island is the comforting home everyone longs for, especially after having been away too long.

Gulf Coast Cottage — Design Q114

Breathtaking sunsets. Sultry summer nights. The glow of the moon and starry skies—romance. Fireflies glowing in the dark, children laughing, playing in the park, the warmth of a hand holding mine, the tenderness of a first kiss—all the joys of a lifetime. Remembered from the porch of the Gulf Coast Cottage.

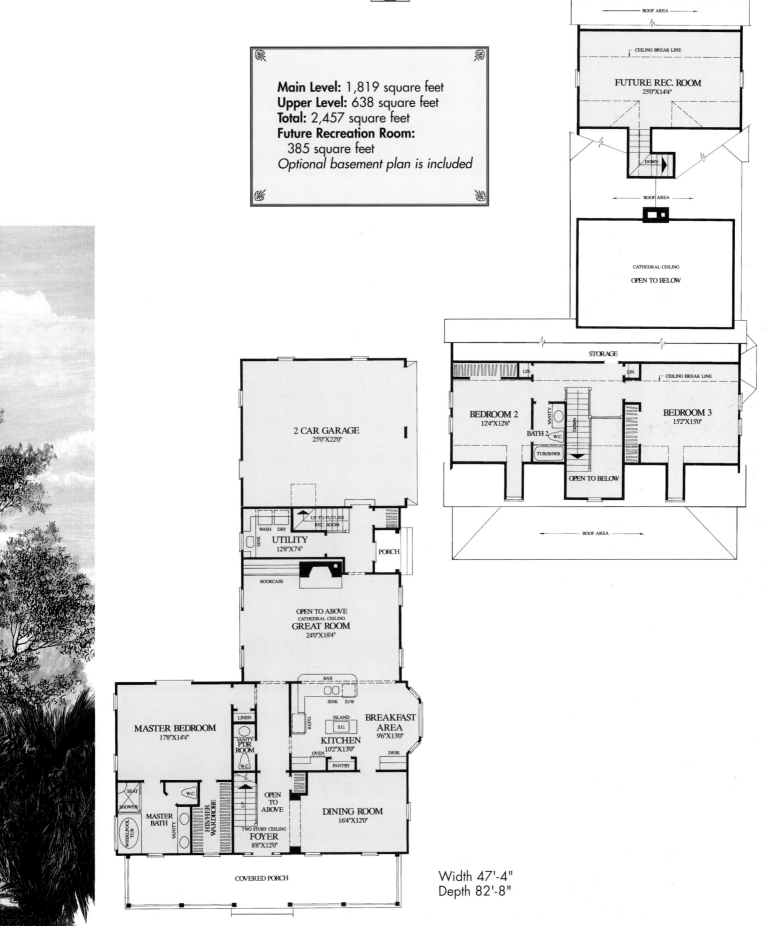

Main Level: 1,819 square feet
Upper Level: 638 square feet
Total: 2,457 square feet
Future Recreation Room:
  385 square feet
Optional basement plan is included

ROOF AREA

CEILING BREAK LINE

FUTURE REC. ROOM
25'0"X14'4"

DOWN

ROOF AREA

CATHEDRAL CEILING

OPEN TO BELOW

STORAGE

LIN.   LIN.   CEILING BREAK LINE

BEDROOM 2
12'4"X12'6"

VANITY

BATH 2
W.C.

DOWN

TUB/SHWR

OPEN TO BELOW

BEDROOM 3
15'2"X15'0"

ROOF AREA

2 CAR GARAGE
25'0"X22'0"

UP TO FUTURE
REC. ROOM

WASH DRY

SINK

UTILITY
12'8"X7'4"

PORCH

BOOKCASE

OPEN TO ABOVE
CATHEDRAL CEILING
GREAT ROOM
24'0"X18'4"

BAR

SINK D/W

REFG.

ISLAND
S.U.

BREAKFAST
AREA
9'6"X13'0"

DESK

MASTER BEDROOM
17'8"X14'4"

LINEN

VANITY
PDR
ROOM

W.C.

KITCHEN
10'2"X13'0"

OVEN

PANTRY

SEAT

SHOWER

WHIRLPOOL
TUB

MASTER
BATH

VANITY

HIS/HER WARDROBE

W.C.

UP

OPEN
TO
ABOVE

TWO STORY CEILING

FOYER
8'8"X12'0"

DINING ROOM
16'4"X12'0"

COVERED PORCH

Width 47'-4"
Depth 82'-8"

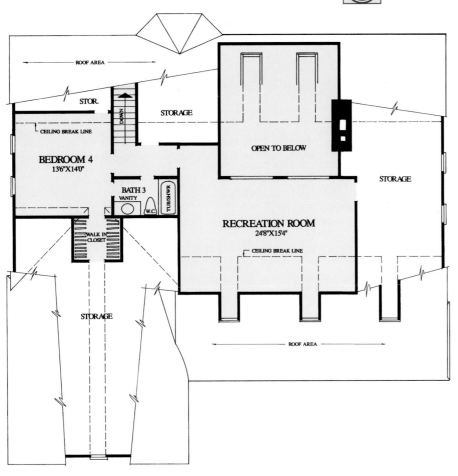

STOR.

STORAGE

ROOF AREA

CEILING BREAK LINE

DOWN

BEDROOM 4
13'6"X14'0"

OPEN TO BELOW

STORAGE

BATH 3
VANITY

TUB/SHWR

W.C.

WALK IN CLOSET

RECREATION ROOM
24'8"X15'4"

CEILING BREAK LINE

STORAGE

ROOF AREA

Square Footage: 2,151
Optional Upper Level:
814 square feet
Optional basement plan is included

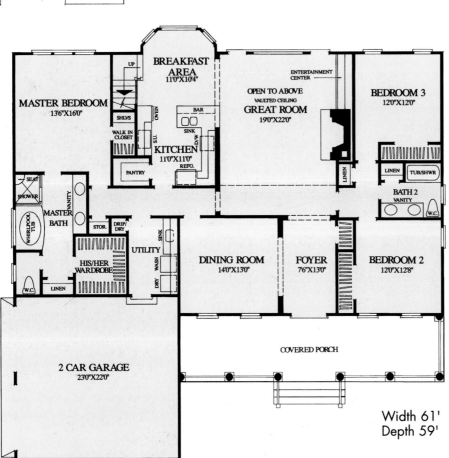

UP

BREAKFAST AREA
11'0"X10'4"

ENTERTAINMENT CENTER

MASTER BEDROOM
13'6"X16'0"

SHLVS

OVEN

BAR

WALK IN CLOSET

SINK

D/W

OPEN TO ABOVE
VAULTED CEILING
GREAT ROOM
19'0"X22'0"

BEDROOM 3
12'0"X12'0"

KITCHEN
11'0"X11'0"

REFG.

PANTRY

LINEN

LINEN

TUB/SHWR

BATH 2
VANITY

W.C.

SEAT

SHOWER

WHIRLPOOL TUB

MASTER BATH

VANITY

STOR.

DRIP/DRY

UTILITY

SINK

WASH

DRY

DINING ROOM
14'0"X13'0"

FOYER
7'6"X13'0"

BEDROOM 2
12'0"X12'8"

W.C.

HIS/HER WARDROBE

LINEN

2 CAR GARAGE
23'0"X22'0"

COVERED PORCH

Width 61'
Depth 59'

Eastern Shore Cottage—Design Q115

Being of incisive line, thought, style and effect, the understated appeal of the Eastern Shore Cottage is reminiscent of a simpler life. Times when neighbor greeted neighbor, doors were left unlocked and a helping hand was near. We can have that again. Choose your neighborhood, plan your home—you've made a wise decision.

Cape Cod Cottage—Design Q116

A soft breeze blowing in from the sea lightly ruffles your hair as you sit on the beach listening to the nearby sound of gulls soaring overhead, recalling the wonderful summers you spent here as a child. Borrowing from the essence and style of Cape Cod—a place that captures your heart—your dream is now a reality. A cozy cottage to call your own, embellished with weathered blue shutters and surrounded with a white picket fence. Your Cape Cod Cottage with its welcoming warmth is a grand place to call "home".

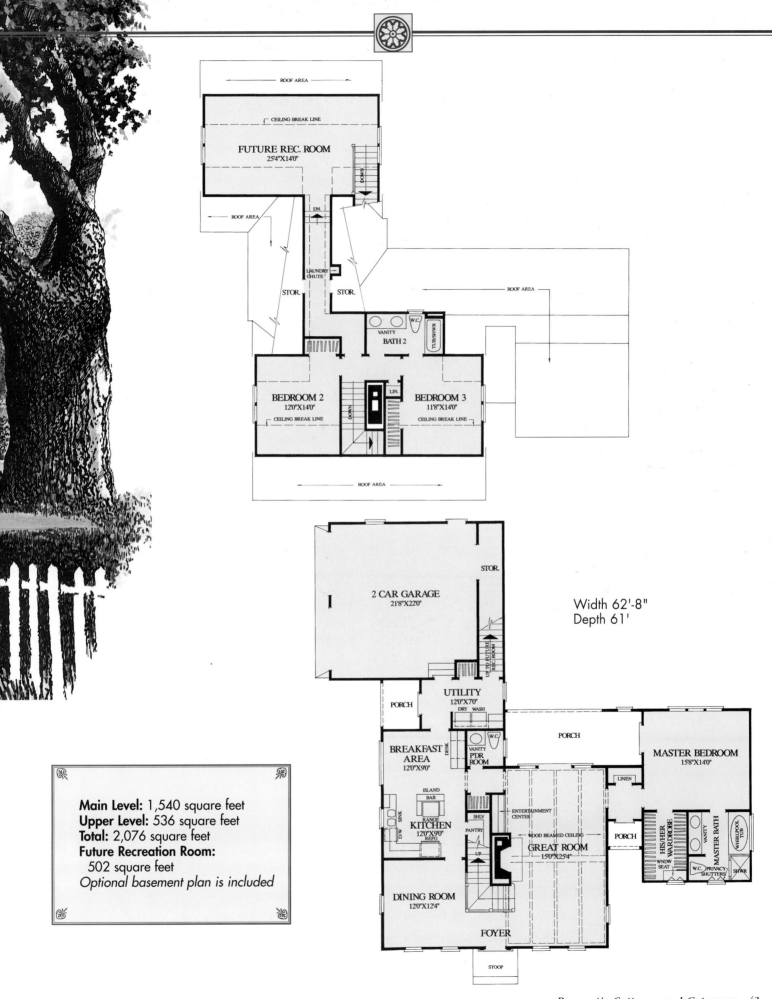

ROOF AREA

CEILING BREAK LINE

FUTURE REC. ROOM
25'4"X14'0"

DOWN

ROOF AREA

DN.

LAUNDRY CHUTE

STOR.

STOR.

ROOF AREA

W.C.

VANITY

TUB/SHWR

BATH 2

BEDROOM 2
12'0"X14'0"

LIN.

DOWN

BEDROOM 3
11'8"X14'0"

CEILING BREAK LINE

CEILING BREAK LINE

ROOF AREA

STOR.

2 CAR GARAGE
21'8"X22'0"

Width 62'-8"
Depth 61'

UP TO FUTURE REC. ROOM

UTILITY
12'0"X7'0"

DRY   WASH

PORCH

W.C.

PORCH

MASTER BEDROOM
15'8"X14'0"

BREAKFAST AREA
12'0"X9'0"

DESK

VANITY

PDR ROOM

ISLAND BAR

D.W.   SINK

RANGE

KITCHEN
12'0"X9'0"

REFG.

PANTRY

SHLV.

UP

ENTERTAINMENT CENTER

WOOD BEAMED CEILING

GREAT ROOM
15'0"X25'4"

LINEN

HIS/HER WARDROBE

VANITY

MASTER BATH

WHIRLPOOL TUB

W.C.   PRIVACY SHUTTERS

SHWR.

WNDW SEAT

PORCH

DINING ROOM
12'0"X12'4"

FOYER

STOOP

Main Level: 1,540 square feet
Upper Level: 536 square feet
Total: 2,076 square feet
Future Recreation Room:
 502 square feet
Optional basement plan is included

Colonial Cottage—Design Q117

Akin to stars and stripes, apple pie—an American tradition—that is what our Colonial Cottage is. No two are ever exactly alike, yet a similarity of classical details exist that strongly tie these cottages together. Try this one on for size—reveal your All-American spirit—you'll be glad you did.

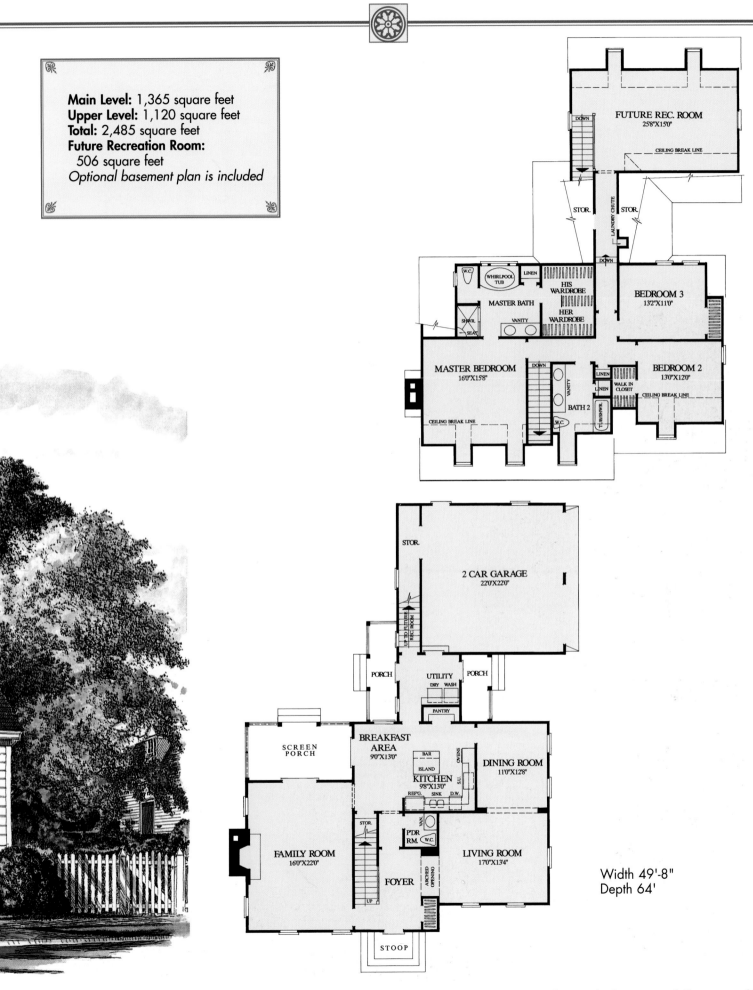

Main Level: 1,365 square feet
Upper Level: 1,120 square feet
Total: 2,485 square feet
Future Recreation Room:
  506 square feet
Optional basement plan is included

FUTURE REC. ROOM
25'8"X15'0"

CEILING BREAK LINE

DOWN

STOR.   STOR.

LAUNDRY CHUTE

W.C.

WHIRLPOOL
TUB   LINEN

HIS
WARDROBE

BEDROOM 3
13'2"X11'0"

MASTER BATH

HER
WARDROBE

SHWR.   VANITY

SEAT

DOWN

MASTER BEDROOM
16'0"X15'8"

DOWN

VANITY

LINEN

LINEN   WALK IN
CLOSET

BEDROOM 2
13'0"X12'0"

CEILING BREAK LINE

BATH 2

CEILING BREAK LINE

W.C.

TUB/SHWR.

STOR.

2 CAR GARAGE
22'0"X22'0"

UP TO FUTURE REC. ROOM

PORCH   UTILITY   PORCH

DRY   WASH

PANTRY

SCREEN
PORCH

BREAKFAST
AREA
9'0"X13'0"

BAR

ISLAND

OVENS

DINING ROOM
11'0"X12'8"

KITCHEN
9'8"X13'0"

REF'G.   SINK   D.W.

STOR.

VAN.

FAMILY ROOM
16'0"X22'0"

P'DR
RM.   W.C.

LIVING ROOM
17'0"X13'4"

FOYER

ARCHED
OPENING

UP

STOOP

Width 49'-8"
Depth 64'

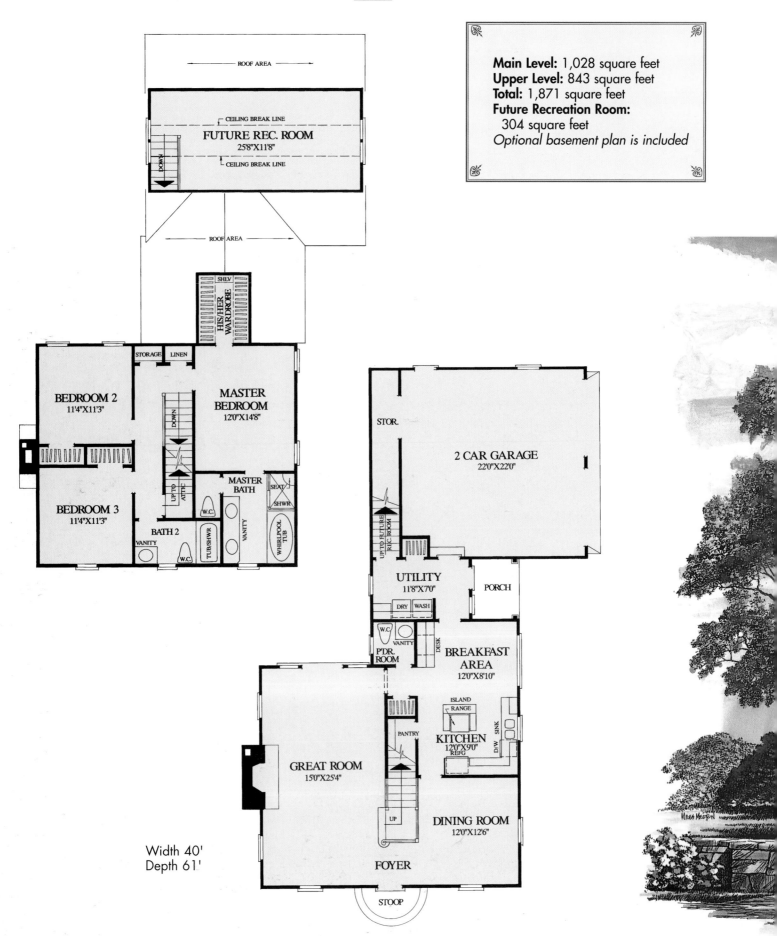

ROOF AREA

FUTURE REC. ROOM
25'8"X11'8"

CEILING BREAK LINE

CEILING BREAK LINE

DOWN

ROOF AREA

Main Level: 1,028 square feet
Upper Level: 843 square feet
Total: 1,871 square feet
Future Recreation Room:
304 square feet
Optional basement plan is included

SHLV

HIS/HER WARDROBE

STORAGE   LINEN

BEDROOM 2
11'4"X11'3"

MASTER BEDROOM
12'0"X14'8"

DOWN

UP TO ATTIC

MASTER BATH

SEAT

SHWR

BEDROOM 3
11'4"X11'3"

W.C.

VANITY

WHIRLPOOL TUB

BATH 2

VANITY

TUB/SHWR

W.C.

STOR.

2 CAR GARAGE
22'0"X22'0"

UP TO FUTURE REC. ROOM

UTILITY
11'8"X7'0"

PORCH

DRY   WASH

W.C.

VANITY

DESK

BREAKFAST AREA
12'0"X8'10"

P'DR. ROOM

ISLAND

RANGE

KITCHEN
12'0"X9'0"

SINK

D/W

REFG

PANTRY

GREAT ROOM
15'0"X25'4"

UP

DINING ROOM
12'0"X12'6"

FOYER

Width 40'
Depth 61'

STOOP

Kentucky Bluegrass—Design Q118

The wind blows gently across the billowing grass. The colts and fillies frolic in the pasture. The gleaming white fences define the checkerboard spaces where this annual rite of spring progresses. From our breakfast nook window, we watch the seasons come and go in our Kentucky Bluegrass home.

Guilford—Design Q119

A New England Saltbox is solid, sturdy, handsome, of clean design and is equally at home on the rugged coast, in the quaint villages or amid the rolling countryside. The Guilford, with its simplicity, proves that less is more. It's definitely understated, but what is left unsaid is of far more importance.

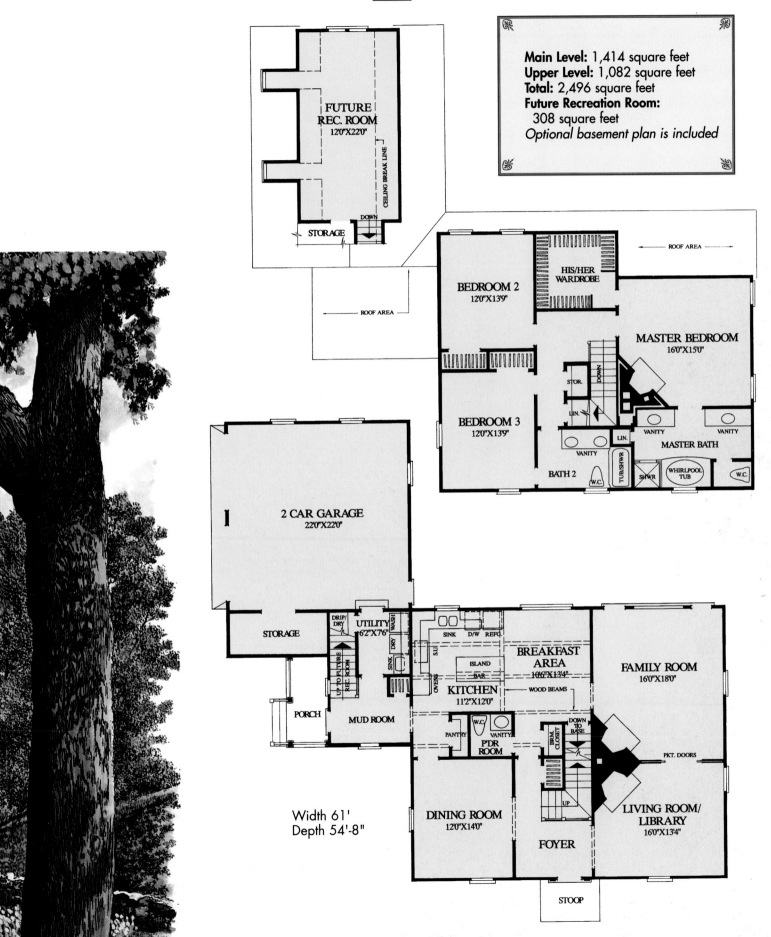

FUTURE
REC. ROOM
12'0"X22'0"

CEILING BREAK LINE

DOWN

STORAGE

Main Level: 1,414 square feet
Upper Level: 1,082 square feet
Total: 2,496 square feet
Future Recreation Room:
  308 square feet
Optional basement plan is included

ROOF AREA

ROOF AREA

BEDROOM 2
12'0"X13'9"

HIS/HER
WARDROBE

MASTER BEDROOM
16'0"X15'0"

STOR.

DOWN

BEDROOM 3
12'0"X13'9"

LIN.

LIN.

VANITY

VANITY

VANITY

MASTER BATH

BATH 2

W.C.

TUB/SHWR

SHWR

WHIRLPOOL
TUB

W.C.

2 CAR GARAGE
22'0"X22'0"

STORAGE

DRIP/
DRY

UTILITY
6'2"X7'6"

WASH

SINK

D/W

REFG.

BREAKFAST
AREA
10'6"X13'4"

FAMILY ROOM
16'0"X18'0"

DRY

SINK

S.U.

OVENS

ISLAND
BAR

KITCHEN
11'2"X12'0"

WOOD BEAMS

UP TO FUTURE
REC. ROOM

DOWN
TO
BASE

PKT. DOORS

PORCH

MUD ROOM

PANTRY

W.C.

VANITY

PDR
ROOM

BR.M.
CLOSET

Width 61'
Depth 54'-8"

DINING ROOM
12'0"X14'0"

UP

LIVING ROOM/
LIBRARY
16'0"X13'4"

FOYER

STOOP

Legendary Hometown Hospitality

*I*n *Legendary Hometown Hospitality, each of the homes have one thing in common—all have gracious entrances. Renowned for warm, genuine welcomes—Southern hospitality was, and is, a ritual of exquisite courtesy.*

For example, The Homestead (page 72) speaks to a quiet lifestyle. This inviting plan is graced with a porch that shelters the home and wraps it in enveloping comfort—with room for a porch swing to share with a family member, best friend, or well-loved pet. Snug and secure, this home provides a just-right spot for reading or daydreaming.

The Palmetto (page 74) offers twice the pleasure of a covered porch. Generous space allows room on the first floor for rocking chairs and lemonade socials with family and friends. The second-floor's covered porch caters to more reflective moments—the perfect place to enjoy a steaming cup of strong coffee or fragrant tea, and your favorite periodical.

The Wyndham (page 78) is undeniably built for living. It's also a home that celebrates the holidays with style. Every Christmas eve, a decorated tree—illuminated with lights—is placed on the upper balcony where grandfather, dressed as Scrooge, throws homemade, wrapped toffee to children below. The family, dressed as Dickens' characters, invites friends and neighbors in for a warming cup of spiced cider. It is a holiday tradition that everyone remembers fondly and looks forward to year after year.

Take time to examine all of the homes in this chapter. You'll find that each one is enhanced with exteriors and floor plans that extend a warm, hospitable welcome to family and friends alike.

Thistlewood—Design Q120

*I*f fairy tales are to be believed, and of course they are, then The Thistlewood captures imaginations of romance and brings memories of delightful cottages and their stories to mind—Goldilocks and the Three Bears, Little Red Riding Hood, Snow White and the Seven Dwarfs, and Jack and the Beanstalk to name a few. The romance. The charm. The detail. What a delightful home—The Thistlewood.

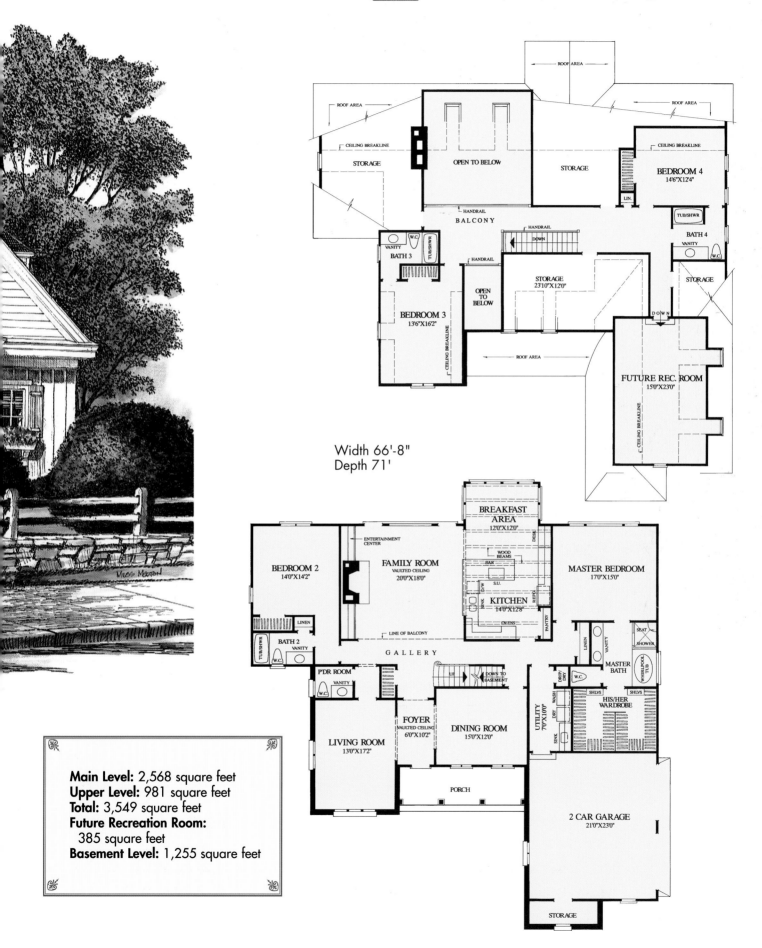

Width 66'-8"
Depth 71'

ROOF AREA

ROOF AREA

ROOF AREA

STORAGE

OPEN TO BELOW

STORAGE

CEILING BREAKLINE

BEDROOM 4
14'6"X12'4"

LIN.

TUB/SHWR

BATH 4

VANITY

W.C.

CEILING BREAKLINE

HANDRAIL

BALCONY

HANDRAIL

DOWN

VANITY

W.C.

BATH 3

TUB/SHWR

HANDRAIL

STORAGE
23'10"X12'0"

STORAGE

OPEN TO BELOW

DOWN

BEDROOM 3
13'6"X16'2"

CEILING BREAKLINE

ROOF AREA

FUTURE REC. ROOM
15'0"X23'0"

CEILING BREAKLINE

BREAKFAST AREA
12'0"X12'0"

DESK

ENTERTAINMENT CENTER

FAMILY ROOM
VAULTED CEILING
20'0"X18'0"

WOOD BEAMS

BAR

S.U.

D.W.

KITCHEN
14'0"X12'8"

REF/R.

MASTER BEDROOM
17'0"X15'0"

BEDROOM 2
14'0"X14'2"

LINEN

SINK

OVENS

PANTRY

TUB/SHWR

BATH 2

VANITY

W.C.

LINE OF BALCONY

GALLERY

LINEN

VANITY

SEAT

SHOWER

MASTER BATH

WHIRLPOOL TUB

P'DR ROOM

VANITY

W.C.

UP

DOWN TO BASEMENT

DRIP/DRY

W.C.

SHLVS

SHLVS

UTILITY
7'0"X10'0"

WASH

DRY

SINK

HIS/HER WARDROBE

LIVING ROOM
13'0"X17'2"

FOYER
VAULTED CEILING
6'0"X10'2"

DINING ROOM
15'0"X12'0"

PORCH

2 CAR GARAGE
21'0"X23'0"

STORAGE

Main Level: 2,568 square feet
Upper Level: 981 square feet
Total: 3,549 square feet
Future Recreation Room:
  385 square feet
Basement Level: 1,255 square feet

Country Cottage—Design Q121

Every neighborhood has the perfect little Country Cottage just down the lane, all tucked into the perfect little yard. Simple, warmly detailed and much loved, everyone who passes by feels that they would be greeted with a welcoming smile. When the children visit—which is often—they know that "Mother Goose" awaits with a hug, a nursery rhyme and milk and cookies.

Square Footage: 2,151
Optional Upper Level:
786 square feet
Optional basement plan is included

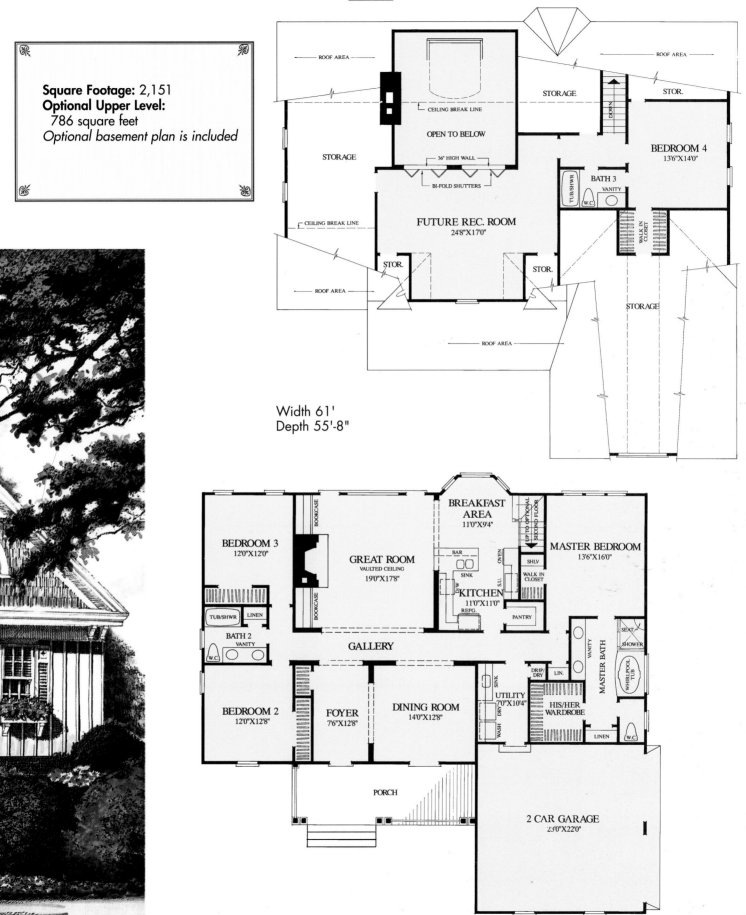

ROOF AREA

ROOF AREA

STORAGE

STOR.

DOWN

STORAGE

CEILING BREAK LINE

OPEN TO BELOW

BEDROOM 4
13'6"X14'0"

STORAGE

36" HIGH WALL

BI-FOLD SHUTTERS

TUB/SHWR

BATH 3

VANITY

W.C

CEILING BREAK LINE

FUTURE REC. ROOM
24'8"X17'0"

WALK IN CLOSET

STOR.

STOR.

STORAGE

ROOF AREA

ROOF AREA

Width 61'
Depth 55'-8"

BOOKCASE

BEDROOM 3
12'0"X12'0"

GREAT ROOM
VAULTED CEILING
19'0"X17'8"

BREAKFAST AREA
11'0"X9'4"

UP TO OPTIONAL SECOND FLOOR

MASTER BEDROOM
13'6"X16'0"

BAR

SINK

OVEN

SHLV

WALK IN CLOSET

BOOKCASE

TUB/SHWR

LINEN

S.U.

S.U.

KITCHEN
11'0"X11'0"

BATH 2

VANITY

D.W

REFG.

PANTRY

W.C

GALLERY

SEAT

SHOWER

VANITY

MASTER BATH

DRIP/DRY

LIN.

WHIRLPOOL TUB

SINK

BEDROOM 2
12'0"X12'8"

FOYER
7'6"X12'8"

DINING ROOM
14'0"X12'8"

UTILITY
7'0"X10'4"

WASH   DRY

HIS/HER WARDROBE

LINEN

W.C

PORCH

2 CAR GARAGE
23'0"X22'0"

Upper Level (Optional)

CATHEDRAL CEILING

ROOF AREA

OPEN TO BELOW

CEILING BREAK LINE

FUTURE
BEDROOM 4
15'6"X12'0"

TUB/SHWR

W.C

FUTURE
BATH 3

VANITY

ROOF AREA

DOWN

HANDRAIL

BALCONY

STORAGE

ROOF AREA

FUTURE REC. ROOM
25'10"X15'0"

STOR.

CEILING BREAK LINE

ROOF AREA

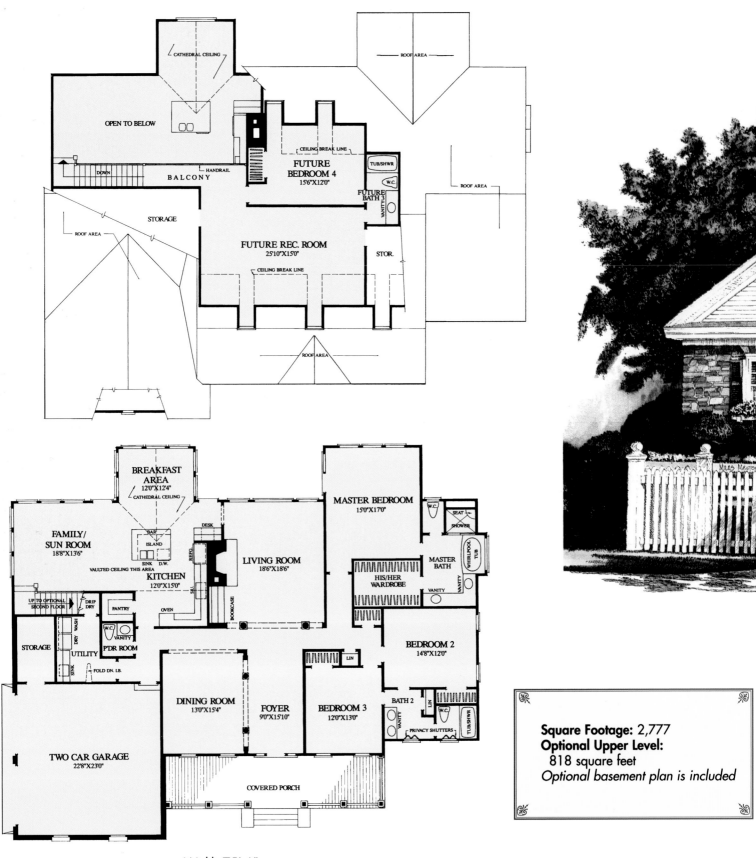

Main Level

BREAKFAST
AREA
12'0"X12'4"
CATHEDRAL CEILING

MASTER BEDROOM
15'0"X17'0"

W.C

SEAT
SHOWER

FAMILY/
SUN ROOM
18'8"X13'6"

BAR
ISLAND
SINK   D.W.

VAULTED CEILING THIS AREA

KITCHEN
12'0"X15'0"

DESK

REFRG.

LIVING ROOM
18'6"X18'6"

MASTER
BATH

WHIRLPOOL
TUB

VANITY

HIS/HER
WARDROBE

UP TO OPTIONAL
SECOND FLOOR

DRIP
DRY

PANTRY

OVEN

BOOKCASE

DRY   WASH

W.C
VANITY

P'DR ROOM

VANITY

STORAGE

UTILITY

SINK

FOLD DN. I.B.

DINING ROOM
13'0"X15'4"

FOYER
9'0"X15'10"

BEDROOM 3
12'0"X13'0"

LIN

BATH 2

LIN

W.C

BEDROOM 2
14'8"X12'0"

TUB/SHWR

VANITY

PRIVACY SHUTTERS

TWO CAR GARAGE
22'8"X23'0"

COVERED PORCH

Width 75'-6"
Depth 60'-2"

Square Footage: 2,777
Optional Upper Level:
   818 square feet
Optional basement plan is included

Bowling Green—Design Q122

Can't you see it now? Sloping green lawns all the way to the river, sprawling wildflower gardens, rose trellises and white fences galore. Children running, playing, calling cheerfully to all who will listen; grown-ups strolling about visiting with one another until—at last, the newlyweds appear for all to toast with good wishes and loving entreaties for their frequent returns. A return to Bowling Green, a place to nestle into, a place called home.

Carlyle—Design Q123

*H*ow special. How perfect. Spiraling smilax, colorful hydrangeas, handsome English box-woods—Southern plantings—for a wonderfully Southern Greek Revival home. The moment we first discovered The Carlyle was a moment to forever cherish. A classical combination for anytime, anywhere. One that will never grow old, because the really good things never do.

Main Level: 1,970 square feet
Upper Level: 660 square feet
Total: 2,630 square feet
Future Recreation Room:
 424 square feet
Optional basement plan is included

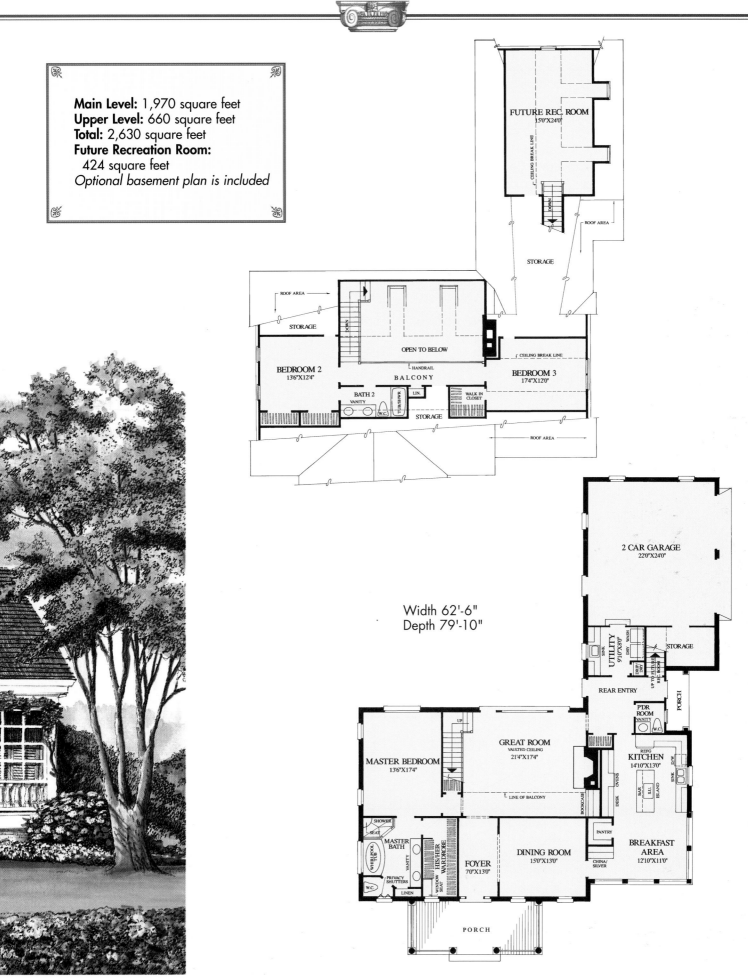

FUTURE REC. ROOM
15'0"X24'0"

CEILING BREAK LINE

DOWN

ROOF AREA

STORAGE

ROOF AREA

STORAGE

DOWN

OPEN TO BELOW

CEILING BREAK LINE

BEDROOM 2
13'6"X12'4"

BALCONY

HANDRAIL

BEDROOM 3
17'4"X12'0"

BATH 2
VANITY

LIN.

TUB/SHWR

W.C.

WALK IN CLOSET

STORAGE

ROOF AREA

2 CAR GARAGE
22'0"X24'0"

Width 62'-6"
Depth 79'-10"

UTILITY
9'10"X8'0"

SINK

DRY WASH

DRY/DRY

UP TO FUTURE REC. ROOM

STORAGE

REAR ENTRY

PORCH

P'DR ROOM
VANITY

W.C.

GREAT ROOM
VAULTED CEILING
21'4"X17'4"

OVENS

DESK

KITCHEN
14'10"X13'0"

REFG

D/W

SINK

MASTER BEDROOM
13'6"X17'4"

UP

LINE OF BALCONY

BOOKCASE

BAR

S.U.

ISLAND

SHOWER
SEAT

MASTER BATH

WHIRLPOOL TUB

PRIVACY SHUTTERS

W.C.

VANITY

HIS/HER WARDROBE

WINDOW SEAT

LINEN

FOYER
7'0"X13'0"

DINING ROOM
15'0"X13'0"

PANTRY

CHINA/SILVER

BREAKFAST AREA
12'10"X11'0"

PORCH

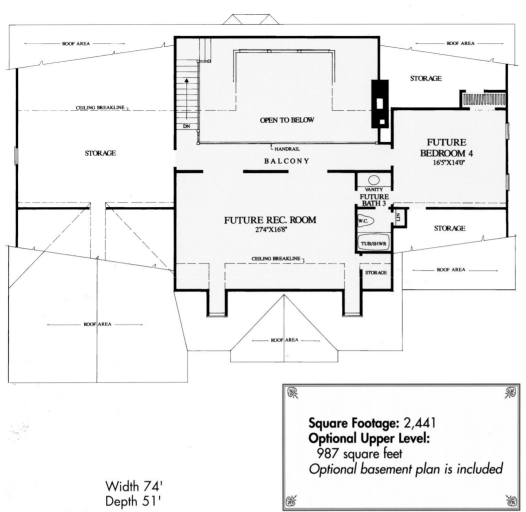

ROOF AREA

ROOF AREA

CEILING BREAKLINE

STORAGE

STORAGE

DN

OPEN TO BELOW

HANDRAIL

BALCONY

FUTURE BEDROOM 4
16'5"X14'0"

VANITY

FUTURE BATH 3

W.C.

FUTURE REC. ROOM
27'4"X16'8"

TUB/SHWR

STORAGE

CEILING BREAKLINE

STORAGE

ROOF AREA

ROOF AREA

ROOF AREA

Width 74'
Depth 51'

Square Footage: 2,441
Optional Upper Level:
  987 square feet
Optional basement plan is included

TUB/SHWR

VANITY

W.C.

BATH 2

VANITY

BEDROOM 3
12'2"X12'0"

UP TO OPTIONAL
SECOND FLOOR

BREAKFAST AREA
11'2"X10'2"

FAMILY ROOM
17'4"X18'8"

BOOKCASE

MASTER BEDROOM
16'0"X15'0"

VAULTED CEILING

BAR

DOWN TO BASE.

SINK

D.W.

LINE OF BALCONY

BEDROOM 2
13'9"X12'0"

SINK

UTILITY

DRY

WASH

PANTRY

OVEN

KITCHEN
14'4"X12'2"

REFG.

S.U.

STORAGE

LIN

W.C.

VANITY

MASTER BATH

WHIRLPOOL TUB

2 CAR GARAGE
22'10"X22'10"

DINING ROOM
12'4"X14'0"

FOYER
7'0"X10'6"

LIVING ROOM
12'0"X16'8"

P'DR ROOM

W.C.

SHELVES

HIS/HER WARDROBE

SHOWER

SEAT

PRIVACY SHUTTERS

PORCH

Camden—Design Q124

The Camden is the home that everyone wants to possess—the one in the neighborhood that never needs to be advertised for sale. Why—because all of your friends have said, "John, if you even think about selling your home, please call me first." And of course, you do. The Camden welcomes each new family to it's hearth with the warmth and glow of home—that special place where the heart is.

Appomattox—Design Q125

If ever a style of residential architecture "spoke to me," it was certainly that of Colonial Virginia. No two houses, though similar in size, shape and detail, are alike. There is always some simple, yet perfect nuance that differs house from house from house. No matter how often I travel among these treasures, there always remains another detail to note—one so subtle as to have gone unseen in prior passings. Tidewater Virginia homes like The Appomattox are strewn along the valleys and waterways of this region and will live on to tell the tales of yet another era in this wonderful land of ours.

ROOF AREA

ROOF AREA

STORAGE

TUB/SHWR

W.C.

BATH 2

VANITY

WALK IN CLOSET

LINEN

W.C.

BATH 3

VANITY

TUB/SHWR

BEDROOM 3
13'8"X12'4"

STORAGE

LINEN

TUB/SHWR

BATH 4

VANITY

W.C.

HANDRAIL

DN

BEDROOM 2
16'0"X14'8"

DN

OPEN TO BELOW

BEDROOM 4
15'0"X11'0"

DN

DN

ROOF AREA

FUTURE REC ROOM
16'0"X32'2"

CEILING BREAK LINE

ROOF AREA

ROOF AREA

ROOF AREA

W.C.

WHIRLPOOL TUB

SEAT

SHOWER

HIS/HER WARDROBE

MASTER BATH

VANITY

VANITY

SCREEN PORCH
VAULTED CEILING

BREAKFAST AREA
VAULTED CEILING
12'2"X9'4"

REFRIG

ENTERTAINMENT CENTER

PANTRY

MASTER BEDROOM
16'0"X17'0"

WALK IN CLOSET

VANITY

W.C.

P'DR ROOM

FAMILY ROOM
19'8"X16'0"

DESK

OVENS

BAR

ISLAND

SINK

D.W.

SINK

KITCHEN
15'0"X16'0"
S.U.

DN TO CELLAR

UP TO FUTURE REC. ROOM

DRIP/DRY

UTILITY
11'0"X9'10"

SINK

LIVING ROOM
16'0"X16'4"

UP

FOYER
VAULTED CEILING
10'8"X14'0"

DINING ROOM
15'0"X14'0"

MUD ROOM

DRY

WASH

BRM CLST

PORCH

PORCH

2 CAR GARAGE
22'0"X22'0"

PORCH

STORAGE

Miles Merton

Width 72'-8"
Depth 67'-6"

Main Level: 2,376 square feet
Upper Level: 1,117 square feet
Total: 3,493 square feet
Future Recreation Room:
  597 square feet
Basement Level: 1,543 square feet

Back Bay Cottage—Design Q126

Near Edisto Island, South Carolina, small back-water communities filled with low-country cottages are dotted here, there and everywhere. Some have manicured lawns. Some have finely raked patterns in the bare, sandy soil. Some are freshly painted and some are so weathered that they appear never to have known the art of cosmetic covering. However, all are abundantly filled with the colors and fragrances of beautiful flowers. There is no doubt that these homes contain many a story. The Back Bay Cottage is clearly well-loved and cared for. Although it bespeaks country, it is with quiet and genteel sophistication.

Main Level: 1,713 square feet
Upper Level: 885 square feet
Total: 2,598 square feet
Future Recreation Room:
    433 square feet
Optional basement plan is included

Width 73'-8"
Depth 46'-8"

Main Level: 2,191 square feet
Upper Level: 1,220 square feet
Total: 3,411 square feet
Future Recreation Room:
  280 square feet
Optional basement plan is included

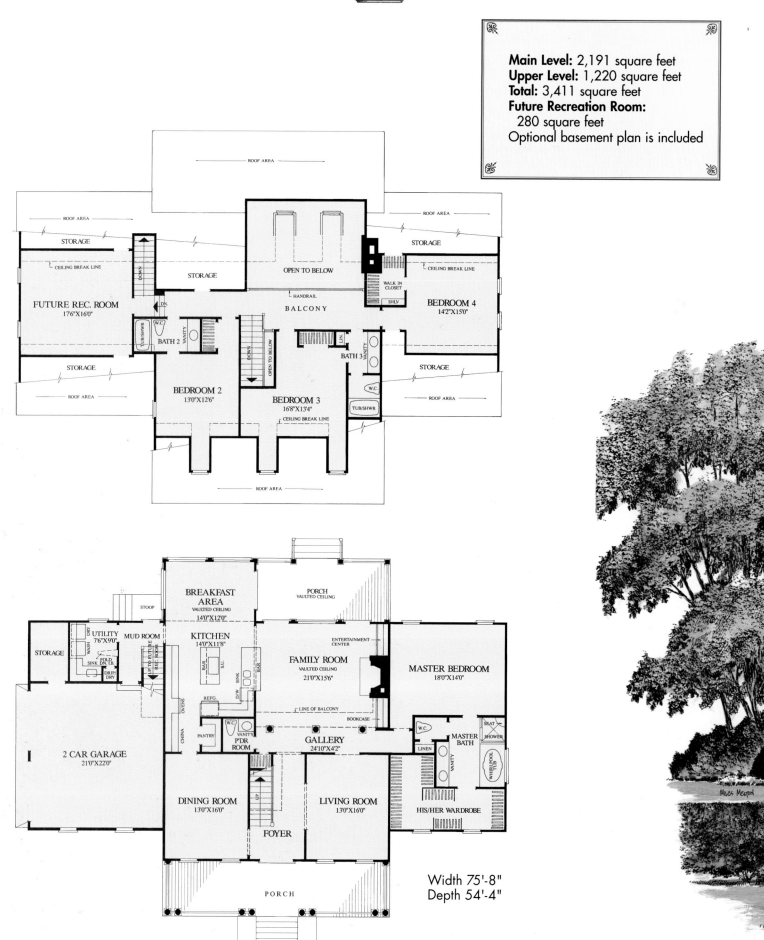

ROOF AREA

ROOF AREA   ROOF AREA

STORAGE   STORAGE

CEILING BREAK LINE   CEILING BREAK LINE

STORAGE   OPEN TO BELOW   WALK IN CLOSET

HANDRAIL   SHLV

FUTURE REC. ROOM
17'6"X16'0"   BALCONY   BEDROOM 4
                                      14'2"X15'0"

TUB/SHWR W.C. BATH 2 VANITY

STORAGE   STORAGE

ROOF AREA   ROOF AREA

BATH 3 VANITY

BEDROOM 2   LIN
13'0"X12'6"   W.C.

BEDROOM 3
16'8"X13'4"   TUB/SHWR

CEILING BREAK LINE

ROOF AREA

BREAKFAST AREA
VAULTED CEILING
14'0"X12'0"   PORCH
                     VAULTED CEILING

STOOP

UTILITY   MUD ROOM   KITCHEN
7'6"X9'0"   14'0"X11'8"   ENTERTAINMENT CENTER

STORAGE   WASH DRY   BAR S.U.   FAMILY ROOM   MASTER BEDROOM
            SINK FOLD DN. TB.   VAULTED CEILING   18'0"X14'0"
            DRIP/DRY   SINK BAR   21'0"X15'6"

            UP TO FUTURE REC. ROOM

            OVENS REFG. D/W   LINE OF BALCONY

            CHINA   BOOKCASE   W.C.

                    PANTRY W.C.   SEAT SHOWER
                                                       MASTER BATH
2 CAR GARAGE   P'DR VANITY   GALLERY   LINEN
21'0"X22'0"   ROOM   24'10"X4'2"   VANITY WHIRLPOOL TUB

DINING ROOM   UP   LIVING ROOM
13'0"X16'0"   13'0"X16'0"   HIS/HER WARDROBE

            FOYER

PORCH

Width 75'-8"
Depth 54'-4"

Biloxi — Design Q127

*A*ll along the Gulf Coast highway one cannot help but admire the beautiful homes that seemingly go on forever. Shingled cottages (with columned porches sitting amid flowing lawns with large shade trees) hold out an inviting hand to come and dream your dreams right there—in a large old rocking chair with a cool glass of lemonade and an unending view of the sea. Neighbors are friendly, visitors are welcome, "ma'am" and "sir" are the norm and life is good—as it should be, at home in The Biloxi.

Bayou Teche—Design Q128

Way down in New Iberia, Louisiana, there is a home that sits just beyond a marvelous old live oak tree whose limbs are so full and heavy that they have to be supported. Imagine growing up in this sleepy little town near the placid waters of the Bayou Teche, marrying the man of your dreams and moving far away. Now, further imagine returning home in your later years to claim this perfectly proportioned creole cottage as yours. This is exactly what happened in New Iberia and the proud owners are lovingly maintaining this treasure—just as it was...so many years ago.

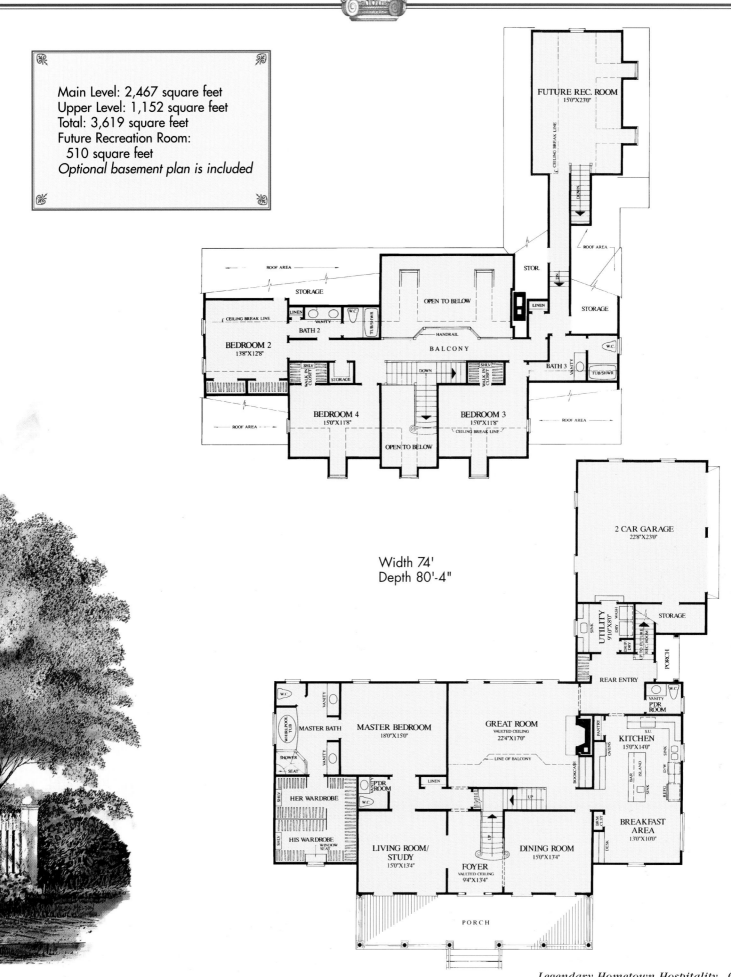

Main Level: 2,467 square feet
Upper Level: 1,152 square feet
Total: 3,619 square feet
Future Recreation Room:
  510 square feet
Optional basement plan is included

FUTURE REC. ROOM
15'0"X23'0"

ROOF AREA

STORAGE

ROOF AREA

OPEN TO BELOW

STOR.

LINEN

STORAGE

LINEN

BATH 2

VANITY

W.C

TUB/SHWR

W.C

BALCONY

HANDRAIL

BEDROOM 2
13'8"X12'8"

BATH 3

VANITY

TUB/SHWR

SHLV

WALK IN CLOSET

STORAGE

DOWN

WALK IN CLOSET

SHLV

ROOF AREA

BEDROOM 4
15'0"X11'8"

BEDROOM 3
15'0"X11'8"

OPEN TO BELOW

2 CAR GARAGE
22'8"X23'0"

Width 74'
Depth 80'-4"

STORAGE

UTILITY
9'10"X8'0"

SINK

DRY WASH

DRIP DRY

UP TO FUTURE REC. ROOM

PORCH

REAR ENTRY

VANITY

W.C

P'DR ROOM

W.C

VANITY

MASTER BEDROOM
18'0"X15'0"

GREAT ROOM
VAULTED CEILING
22'4"X17'0"

PANTRY

OVENS

S.U.

KITCHEN
15'0"X14'0"

MASTER BATH

WHIRLPOOL TUB

SHOWER

SEAT

VANITY

LINE OF BALCONY

LINEN

BAR

ISLAND

SINK

D.W

REFG.

SINK

P'DR ROOM

VANITY

W.C

SHLV

HER WARDROBE

BOOKCASE

BRM CLST

DESK

BREAKFAST AREA
13'0"X10'0"

SHLV

HIS WARDROBE

WINDOW SEAT

LIVING ROOM/ STUDY
15'0"X13'4"

FOYER
VAULTED CEILING
9'4"X13'4"

UP

DINING ROOM
15'0"X13'4"

PORCH

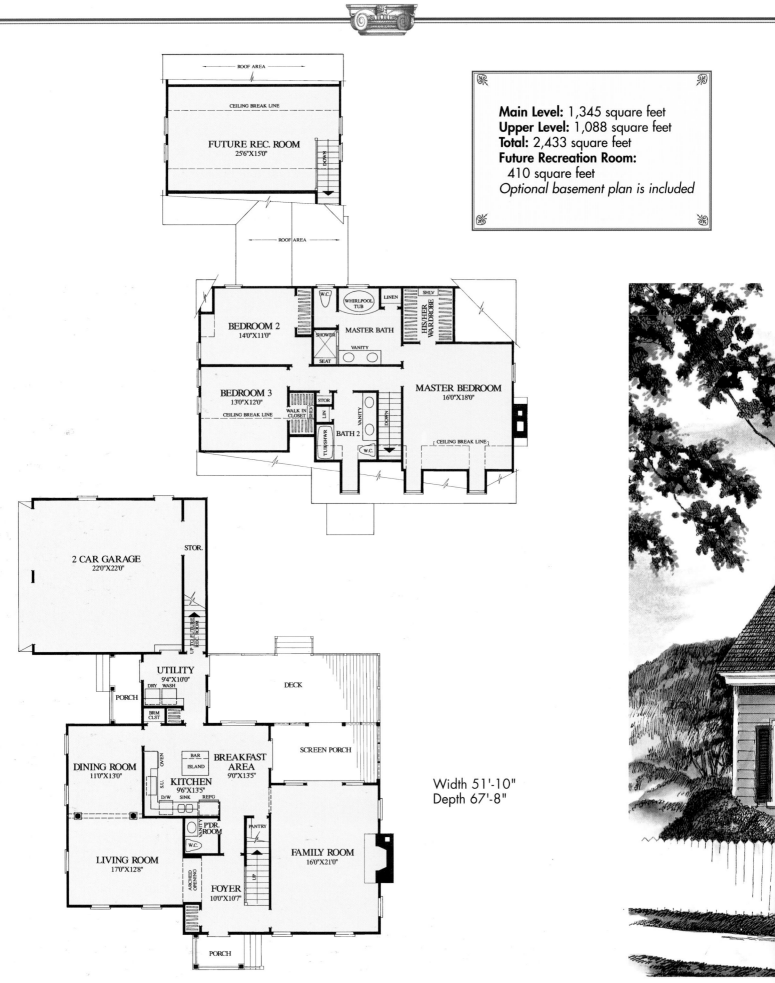

ROOF AREA

CEILING BREAK LINE

FUTURE REC. ROOM
25'6"X15'0"

DOWN

ROOF AREA

Main Level: 1,345 square feet
Upper Level: 1,088 square feet
Total: 2,433 square feet
Future Recreation Room:
410 square feet
Optional basement plan is included

W.C.

WHIRLPOOL
TUB

LINEN

SHLV

BEDROOM 2
14'0"X11'0"

MASTER BATH

SHOWER

HIS/HER WARDROBE

SEAT

VANITY

BEDROOM 3
13'0"X12'0"

STOR

MASTER BEDROOM
16'0"X18'0"

CEILING BREAK LINE

WALK IN CLOSET

SHLV

LIN

VANITY

DOWN

TUB/SHWR

BATH 2

W.C.

CEILING BREAK LINE

2 CAR GARAGE
22'0"X22'0"

STOR.

UP TO FUTURE REC. ROOM

UTILITY
9'4"X10'0"

DECK

DRY   WASH

PORCH

BRM
CLST

SCREEN PORCH

BAR

BREAKFAST AREA
9'0"X13'5"

DINING ROOM
11'0"X13'0"

OVEN

ISLAND

S.U.

KITCHEN
9'6"X13'5"

D/W   SINK   REFG

P'DR. ROOM

PANTRY

Width 51'-10"
Depth 67'-8"

W.C.

VANITY

LIVING ROOM
17'0"X12'8"

ARCHED OPENING

FAMILY ROOM
16'0"X21'0"

FOYER
10'0"X10'7"

UP

PORCH

Holly Hock Cottage—Design Q129

After spending the day in New Bern, North Carolina, touring Tryon Palace and larger homes in the historic district, the most pleasant surprise was waiting just around the corner. We were captivated by the sight of the Holly Hock Cottage. The proportions were perfect, the size adorable, the simplicity engaging and the gardens ablaze in irregular charm and color. Feasting our eyes on this little cottage at the end of our stay was an unexpected and heart-warming delight.

Homestead—Design Q130

Rounding a curve near the Blue Ridge Parkway—there, straight ahead, nestled between adjacent ridges lies The Homestead. With a sudden catch in the throat, one is immediately immersed in images of the generations who have lived, loved and toiled there. Lullabies, folk tales and the clear lilt of a fiddle in the crisp evening air invade ones senses in a rush of nostalgic reverie. Imagine the stories that could be told!

Main Level: 1,913 square feet
Upper Level: 997 square feet
Total: 2,910 square feet
Future Recreation Room:
  377 square feet
Optional basement plan is included

ROOF AREA

CEILING BREAK LINE

OPEN TO BELOW

BEDROOM 4
13'0"X11'0"

ROOF AREA

STORAGE

CEILING BREAK LINE

TUB/SHWR

HANDRAIL

BALCONY

LIN.

BATH 2

W.C.

W.C.

FUTURE REC. ROOM
21'0"X17'0"

VANITY

DOWN

VANITY

BATH 3

TUB/SHWR

ROOF AREA

ROOF AREA

BEDROOM 2
13'0"X14'0"

SHLV

WALK IN
CLOSET

BEDROOM 3
13'0"X13'2"

STORAGE

WALK IN
CLOSET

SHLV

CEIL BREAK LINE

ROOF AREA

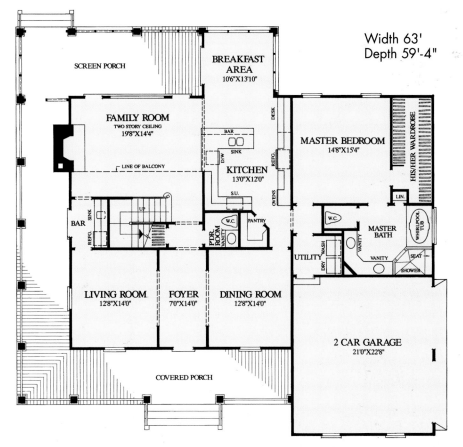

Width 63'
Depth 59'-4"

SCREEN PORCH

BREAKFAST
AREA
10'6"X13'10"

DESK

FAMILY ROOM
TWO STORY CEILING
19'8"X14'4"

BAR

SINK

D/W

MASTER BEDROOM
14'8"X15'4"

HIS/HER WARDROBE

LINE OF BALCONY

REFG.

OVENS

KITCHEN
13'0"X12'0"

S.U.

LIN.

BAR

SINK

UP

PDR.
ROOM
VANITY

W.C.

PANTRY

WHIRLPOOL
TUB

REFG.

W.C.

VANITY

MASTER
BATH

UTILITY

DRY

WASH

VANITY

SEAT

SHOWER

LIVING ROOM
12'8"X14'0"

FOYER
7'0"X14'0"

DINING ROOM
12'8"X14'0"

2 CAR GARAGE
21'0"X22'8"

COVERED PORCH

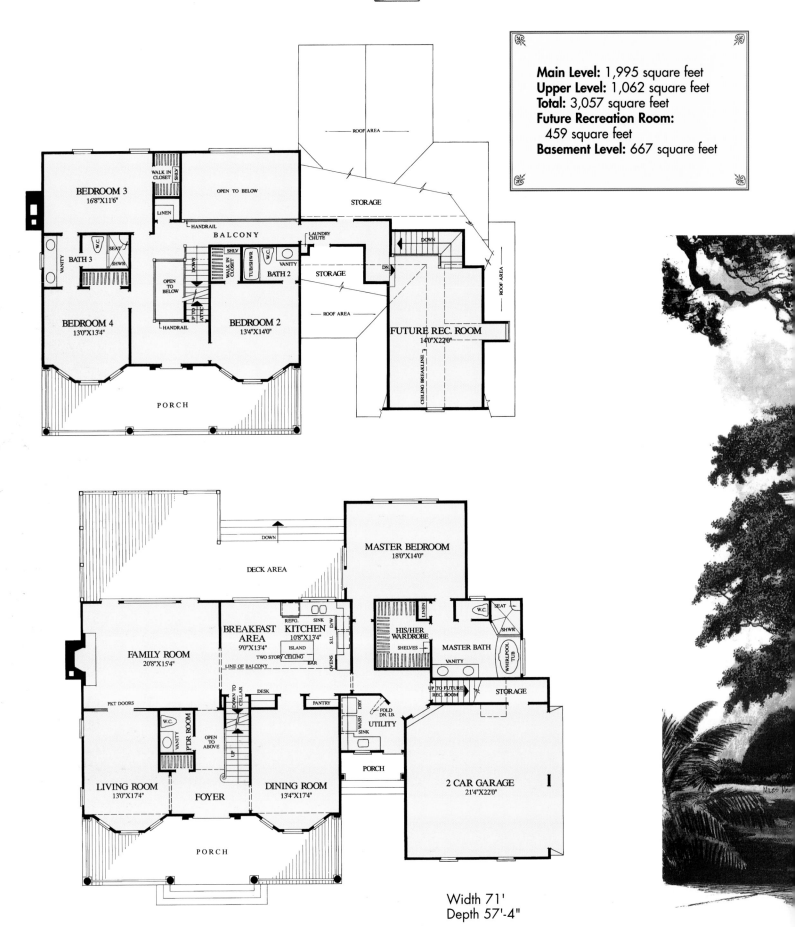

Main Level: 1,995 square feet
Upper Level: 1,062 square feet
Total: 3,057 square feet
Future Recreation Room:
  459 square feet
Basement Level: 667 square feet

ROOF AREA

BEDROOM 3
16'8"X11'6"

OPEN TO BELOW

STORAGE

WALK IN CLOSET

LINEN

HANDRAIL

BALCONY

LAUNDRY CHUTE

DOWN

VANITY

BATH 3

SEAT

SHWR

W.C.

SHLV

TUB/SHWR

W.C.

VANITY

OPEN TO BELOW

WALK IN CLOSET

STORAGE

BATH 2

DN.

ROOF AREA

BEDROOM 4
13'0"X13'4"

HANDRAIL

UP TO ATTIC

BEDROOM 2
13'4"X14'0"

ROOF AREA

FUTURE REC. ROOM
14'0"X22'0"

CEILING BREAKLINE

PORCH

DECK AREA

DOWN

MASTER BEDROOM
18'0"X14'0"

LINEN

W.C.

SEAT

REFG.

SINK

D/W

FAMILY ROOM
20'8"X15'4"

BREAKFAST AREA
9'0"X13'4"

KITCHEN
10'8"X13'4"

HIS/HER WARDROBE

SHWR

TWO STORY CEILING

ISLAND

S.U.

SHELVES

MASTER BATH

VANITY

WHIRLPOOL TUB

LINE OF BALCONY

OVENS

BAR

PKT DOORS

DOWN TO CELLAR

DESK

PANTRY

FOLD DN. LB.

UP TO FUTURE REC. ROOM

STORAGE

W.C.

VANITY

PDR ROOM

OPEN TO ABOVE

UP

WASH

DRY

SINK

UTILITY

2 CAR GARAGE
21'4"X22'0"

LIVING ROOM
13'0"X17'4"

FOYER

DINING ROOM
13'4"X17'4"

PORCH

PORCH

Width 71'
Depth 57'-4"

Palmetto—Design Q131

There is a very special home that sits on a corner of Meeting Street in Charleston, South Carolina. While being overshadowed by larger and more grandiose homes, The Palmetto speaks softly, yet takes no back seat to another. The delicate proportions and simplistic charm of this home purport a simple dignity that captures ones very heart. Is it any wonder that all who return can hardly wait to hear the familiar, "welcome home."

Woodbridge—Design Q132

W andering the back streets of Woodbridge, Connecticut, where we became lost amid all the myriad crooks and turns in the roads, we came upon a perfectly proportioned home. The Woodbridge is so intriguing that we looked, admired, walked on and returned yet again for another admiring glance. With the tolling of the church bells, instant thoughts of being in another era surfaced—thoughts of a simpler time and place.

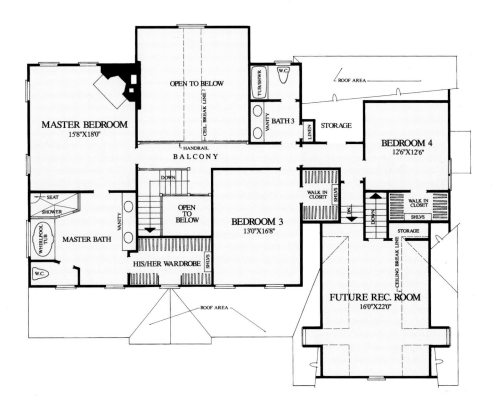

UPPER LEVEL

MASTER BEDROOM
15'8"X18'0"

OPEN TO BELOW

W.C.
TUB/SHWR

BATH 3

VANITY

ROOF AREA

LINEN

STORAGE

BEDROOM 4
12'6"X12'6"

BALCONY

HANDRAIL

SEAT

SHOWER

DOWN

VANITY

OPEN TO BELOW

WALK IN CLOSET

SHLVS

WALK IN CLOSET

SHLVS

WHIRLPOOL TUB

MASTER BATH

BEDROOM 3
13'0"X16'8"

DOWN

STORAGE

W.C.

HIS/HER WARDROBE

SHLVS

FUTURE REC. ROOM
16'0"X22'0"

ROOF AREA

Width 63'-4"
Depth 51'

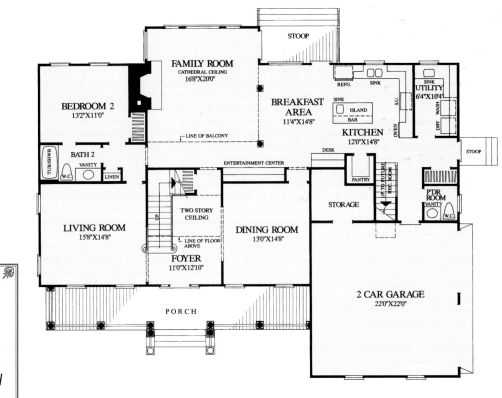

MAIN LEVEL

STOOP

FAMILY ROOM
CATHEDRAL CEILING
16'8"X20'0"

REFG.

SINK

UTILITY
6'4"X10'4"

BEDROOM 2
13'2"X11'0"

BREAKFAST AREA
11'4"X14'8"

SINK

ISLAND

BAR

KITCHEN
12'0"X14'8"

OVEN

WASH

DRY

STOOP

LINE OF BALCONY

DESK

BATH 2

VANITY

W.C.

LINEN

ENTERTAINMENT CENTER

PANTRY

STORAGE

UP TO FUTURE REC. ROOM

P'DR ROOM

VANITY

W.C.

LIVING ROOM
15'8"X14'8"

UP

TWO STORY CEILING

LINE OF FLOOR ABOVE

DINING ROOM
13'0"X14'8"

STORAGE

2 CAR GARAGE
22'0"X22'0"

FOYER
11'0"X12'10"

PORCH

Main Level: 1,876 square feet
Upper Level: 1,396 square feet
Total: 3,272 square feet
Future Recreation Room:
  405 square feet
Optional basement plan is included

Wyndham—Design Q133

Vintage, yet new—The Wyndham looks seasoned, yet functions for today. It starts out looking good and stays that way. This is a home that was considered "in" in years past, "in" now, and will be "in" years from now. Every neighborhood has a Georgian classic that demands respect and this is just such a house—so stately with the columned porches to the front of the impressive main body, so circumspect in the correctness of detail, so perfect in every sense of the word.

Main Level: 2,416 square feet
Upper Level: 1,535 square feet
Total: 3,951 square feet
Future Recreation Room:
  552 square feet
Optional basement plan is included

ROOF AREA

STORAGE

TUB/SHWR
VANITY
W.C.   BATH 2
VANITY

BEDROOM 3
14'0"X12'0"

WALK IN CLOSET
SHLV   WALK IN CLOSET

BEDROOM 4
15'0"X13'8"

CEILING BREAK LINE

DOWN

FUTURE REC. ROOM
22'0"X18'8"

DN.

STOR.

SHLV   WALK IN CLOSET   STORAGE

VANITY   LIN.

W.C.   BATH 3

LIN.   SHLV   WALK IN CLOSET

OPEN TO BELOW
HANDRAIL
BALCONY

ROOF AREA

BEDROOM 2
15'0"X15'0"

OPEN TO BELOW

BEDROOM 5
15'0"X13'8"

ROOF AREA

W.C.
VANITY

MASTER BATH

WHIRLPOOL TUB

VANITY

MASTER BEDROOM
14'0"X18'0"

LIN.

SHOWER SEAT

HIS/HER WARDROBE

STORAGE

WASH DRY   DRIP/DRY

UTILITY
8'4"X 8'10"
SINK

UP TO FUTURE REC. ROOM

2 CAR GARAGE
22'0"X23'0"

MUD ROOM

PORCH   STOR.

BUTLERS PANTRY
DESK

SINK D/W   REFG
SINK   S.U.

ISLAND
BAR

OVEN   KITCHEN
14'0"X12'0"

PANTRY

BREAKFAST AREA
11'4"X12'0"

UP

OPEN TO ABOVE

FAMILY ROOM
15'0"X22'0"

P'DR ROOM
W.C.   VANITY

LINE OF BALCONY

FOYER
TWO STORY CEILING
14'0"X15'0"

DINING ROOM
15'0"X12'0"

LIVING ROOM
15'0"X15'0"

PORCH

Width 77'-6"
Depth 63'-6"

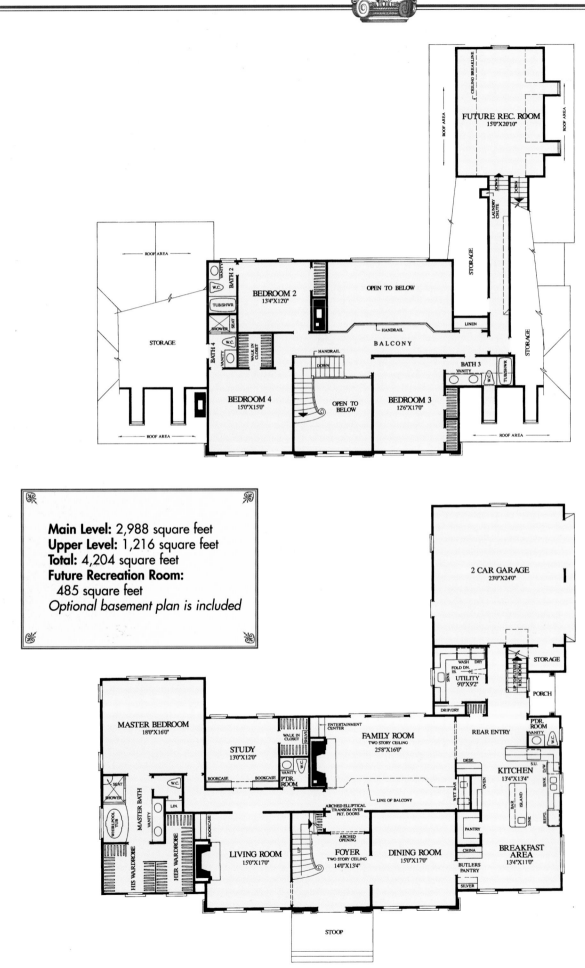

FUTURE REC. ROOM
15'0"X20'10"

BEDROOM 2
13'4"X12'0"

OPEN TO BELOW

BATH 2

STORAGE

BALCONY

BEDROOM 4
15'0"X15'0"

OPEN TO BELOW

BEDROOM 3
12'6"X17'0"

BATH 3

BATH 4

Main Level: 2,988 square feet
Upper Level: 1,216 square feet
Total: 4,204 square feet
Future Recreation Room:
   485 square feet
Optional basement plan is included

2 CAR GARAGE
23'0"X24'0"

UTILITY
9'0"X9'2"

STORAGE

PORCH

P'DR.
ROOM

REAR ENTRY

MASTER BEDROOM
18'0"X16'0"

STUDY
13'0"X12'0"

WALK IN CLOSET

ENTERTAINMENT CENTER

FAMILY ROOM
TWO STORY CEILING
25'8"X16'0"

KITCHEN
13'4"X13'4"

DESK

P'DR. ROOM

MASTER BATH

WHIRLPOOL TUB

SHOWER

HIS WARDROBE

HER WARDROBE

BOOKCASE

LIVING ROOM
15'0"X17'0"

FOYER
TWO STORY CEILING
14'0"X13'4"

ARCHED ELLIPTICAL
TRANSOM OVER
PKT. DOORS

ARCHED OPENING

DINING ROOM
15'0"X17'0"

WET BAR

PANTRY

CHINA

BUTLERS PANTRY

SILVER

BREAKFAST AREA
13'4"X11'0"

LINE OF BALCONY

STOOP

Width 83'
Depth 70'-4"

The Providence—Design Q134

Homes that I have enjoyed in my travels throughout Rhode Island and Connecticut were my inspiration for the Providence. The fine detail found in houses of the Federal (Adams) period such as Palladian windows, fluted pilasters and pedimented entries are all incorporated in this design. What better place to showcase The Providence than in Williamsburg, Virginia—built in the very center of our Colonial heritage. The Providence is also available with a brick exterior and a total square footage of 4,360.

Waverly—Design Q135

The Waverly is a classical Georgian home that, from all appearances, could be either the newest dwelling on the block or the old historic home on whose grounds the surrounding neighborhood was conceived and developed. Proportions and authentic details so handsomely depicted, anchored by twin chimneys—on either side of the impressive center structure, give one reflective pause upon approaching The Waverly for the first time—as well as all the times in the future when feeling truly welcomed home.

Main Level: 2,492 square feet
Upper Level: 1,313 square feet
Total: 3,805 square feet
Future Recreation Room:
  687 square feet
Optional basement plan is included

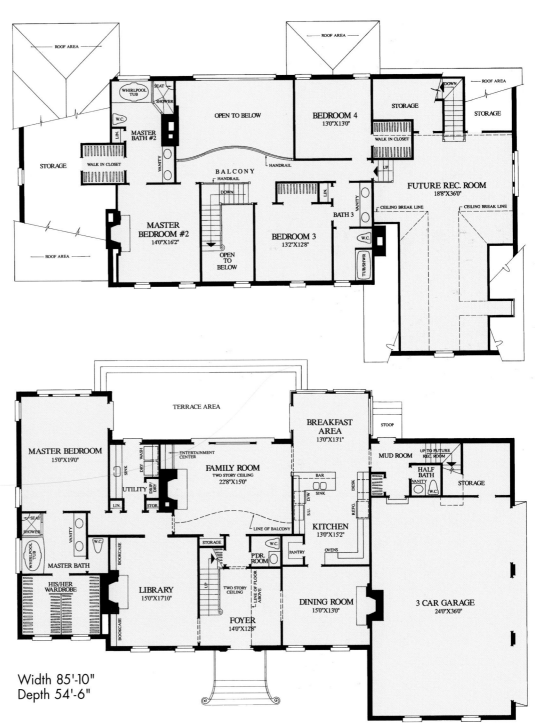

ROOF AREA

ROOF AREA

ROOF AREA

WHIRLPOOL TUB

SEAT

SHOWER

W.C.

LIN.

MASTER BATH #2

VANITY

STORAGE

WALK IN CLOSET

OPEN TO BELOW

BEDROOM 4
13'0"X13'0"

STORAGE

DOWN

ROOF AREA

STORAGE

WALK IN CLOSET

UP

BALCONY

HANDRAIL

HANDRAIL

DOWN

LIN.

VANITY

BATH 3

FUTURE REC. ROOM
18'8"X36'0"

CEILING BREAK LINE

CEILING BREAK LINE

MASTER BEDROOM #2
14'0"X16'2"

ROOF AREA

OPEN TO BELOW

BEDROOM 3
13'2"X12'8"

W.C.

TUB/SHWR

TERRACE AREA

BREAKFAST AREA
13'0"X13'1"

STOOP

MASTER BEDROOM
15'0"X19'0"

SINK

WASH

DRY

ENTERTAINMENT CENTER

LIN.

DRIP DRY

STOR.

UTILITY

FAMILY ROOM
TWO STORY CEILING
22'8"X15'0"

BAR

S.U.

D/W

SINK

LINE OF BALCONY

MUD ROOM

DESK

UP TO FUTURE REC. ROOM

HALF BATH

VANITY

W.C.

STORAGE

SEAT

SHOWER

VANITY

W.C.

WHIRLPOOL TUB

MASTER BATH

BOOKCASE

KITCHEN
13'0"X15'2"

REFG.

HIS/HER WARDROBE

BOOKCASE

LIBRARY
15'0"X17'10"

STORAGE

TWO STORY CEILING

UP

LINE OF FLOOR ABOVE

W.C.

P'DR. ROOM

PANTRY

OVENS

DINING ROOM
15'0"X13'0"

3 CAR GARAGE
24'0"X36'0"

FOYER
14'0"X12'8"

Width 85'-10"
Depth 54'-6"

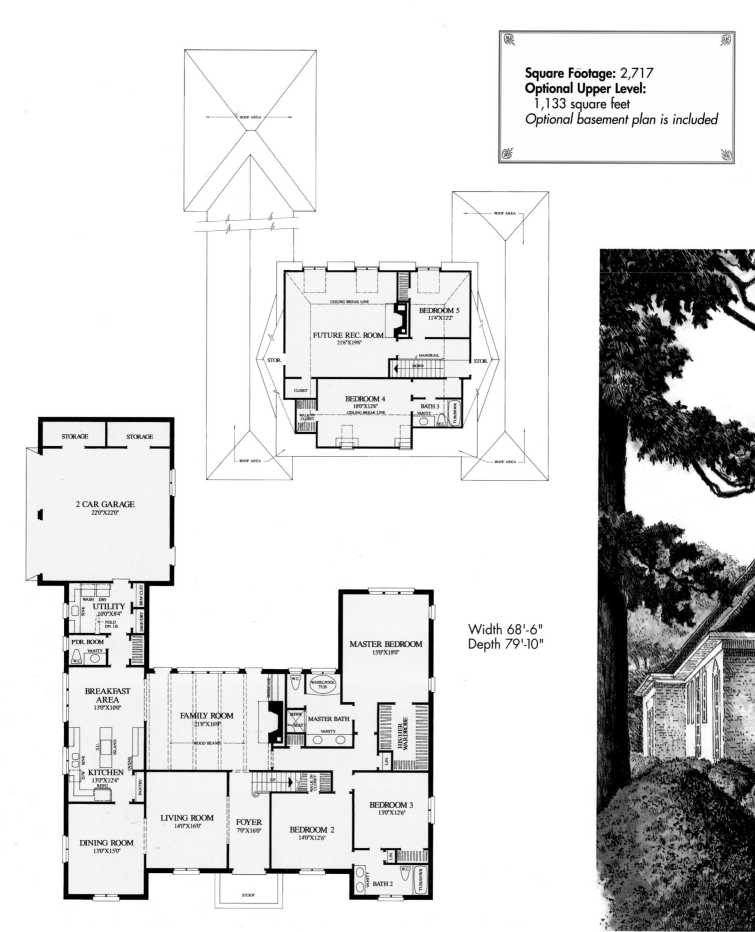

Square Footage: 2,717
Optional Upper Level:
1,133 square feet
Optional basement plan is included

ROOF AREA

ROOF AREA

BEDROOM 5
11'4"X12'2"

FUTURE REC. ROOM
21'6"X19'6"

CEILING BREAK LINE

STOR.

HANDRAIL

DOWN

STOR.

CLOSET

BEDROOM 4
18'0"X12'6"
CEILING BREAK LINE

WALK IN CLOSET

BATH 3
VANITY

W.C.

TUB/SHWR

ROOF AREA

ROOF AREA

STORAGE   STORAGE

2 CAR GARAGE
22'0"X22'0"

WASH DRY

BRM CLST

UTILITY
10'0"X8'4"
FOLD
DN. LB.

SINK

DRIP/DRY

P'DR. ROOM
VANITY
W.C.

BREAKFAST
AREA
13'0"X10'0"

FAMILY ROOM
21'8"X16'0"

WOOD BEAMS

MASTER BEDROOM
15'0"X18'0"

W.C.

WHIRLPOOL
TUB

SINK

S.U. ISLAND

KITCHEN
13'0"X12'4"

OVENS

D.W.

REFG

PANTRY

MASTER BATH
VANITY

SHWR
SEAT

LIN.

HIS/HER
WARDROBE

DINING ROOM
13'0"X15'0"

LIVING ROOM
14'0"X16'0"

FOYER
7'0"X16'0"

UP

WALK IN
CLOSET

BEDROOM 2
14'0"X12'6"

BEDROOM 3
13'0"X12'6"

LIN.

W.C.

VANITY

BATH 2

TUB/SHWR

STOOP

Width 68'-6"
Depth 79'-10"

Lafayette—Design Q136

Let me tell you a little known, but very true story. When our soldiers were overseas during World War I, they fell in love with the inviting, aged and patinaed old homes of France—homes that gave them feelings of warmth in their otherwise desolate days. Upon returning home after the war, they decided to build romantic cottages such as Lafayette for themselves; thus, introducing to our shores the symmetry, quaintness and detail of classical French architecture. And as all classics do, they remain and endure gracefully the test of time.

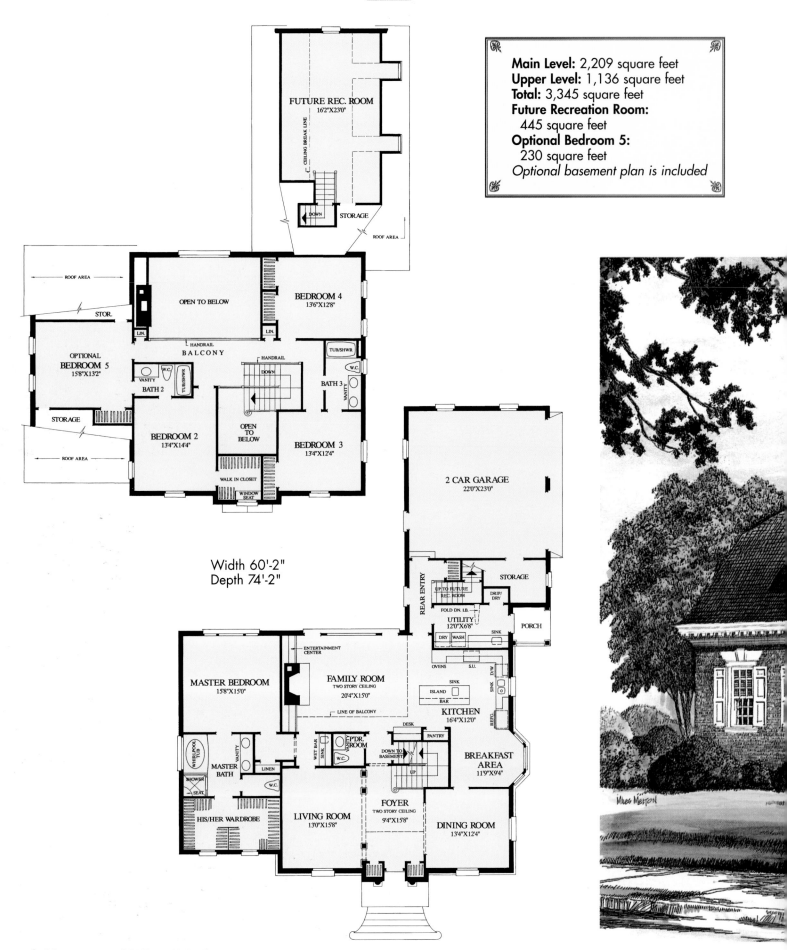

FUTURE REC. ROOM
16'2"X23'0"

CEILING BREAK LINE

DOWN
STORAGE

ROOF AREA

Main Level: 2,209 square feet
Upper Level: 1,136 square feet
Total: 3,345 square feet
Future Recreation Room:
    445 square feet
Optional Bedroom 5:
    230 square feet
Optional basement plan is included

ROOF AREA

STOR.

OPTIONAL
BEDROOM 5
15'8"X13'2"

STORAGE

ROOF AREA

OPEN TO BELOW

BEDROOM 4
13'6"X12'8"

LIN.

LIN.

HANDRAIL
B A L C O N Y

HANDRAIL

TUB/SHWR

W.C.

VANITY

BATH 2

TUB/SHWR

W.C.

DOWN

BATH 3

VANITY

BEDROOM 2
13'4"X14'4"

OPEN
TO
BELOW

BEDROOM 3
13'4"X12'4"

WALK IN CLOSET

WINDOW
SEAT

Width 60'-2"
Depth 74'-2"

2 CAR GARAGE
22'0"X23'0"

REAR ENTRY

STORAGE

UP TO FUTURE
REC. ROOM

DRIP/
DRY

FOLD DN. I.B.

UTILITY
12'0"X6'8"

SINK

PORCH

DRY

WASH

ENTERTAINMENT
CENTER

MASTER BEDROOM
15'8"X15'0"

FAMILY ROOM
TWO STORY CEILING
20'4"X15'0"

OVENS

S.U.

SINK

KITCHEN
16'4"X12'0"

D/W

REFG.

LINE OF BALCONY

ISLAND

BAR

WHIRLPOOL
TUB

VANITY

MASTER
BATH

LINEN

WET BAR

SINK

P'DR.
ROOM

W.C.

DESK

PANTRY

DOWN TO
BASEMENT

BREAKFAST
AREA
11'9"X9'4"

SHOWER

SEAT

W.C.

HIS/HER WARDROBE

LIVING ROOM
13'0"X15'8"

FOYER
TWO STORY CEILING
9'4"X15'8"

UP

DINING ROOM
13'4"X12'4"

Miles Merton

Philadelphia—Design Q137

*O*ur Liberty Bell, Ben Franklin's print shop, the signing of the Declaration of Independence—what history one feels in the streets of Philadelphia. So many beginnings and so many endings in the foundation and growth of our country have their roots in this city. Classical and commanding, The Philadelphia is typical of many homes in the Historic District and would be majestic in any neighborhood anywhere—today as well as yesterday and tomorrow.

Chesapeake Bay—Design Q138

*A*hh...the "Chesapeake Bay." What memories...This private old home on Maryland's Eastern shore, with gracious lawns spreading beyond the porches all the way to the water's edge, is the perfect place for gatherings, garden parties, weddings, afternoon teas, croquet, cookouts and the most tantalizing treat of all—local crabs boiled in spices and served up in buckets as (mallets in hand) one anticipates the noisy, tasty and fun-filled evening with friends and family.

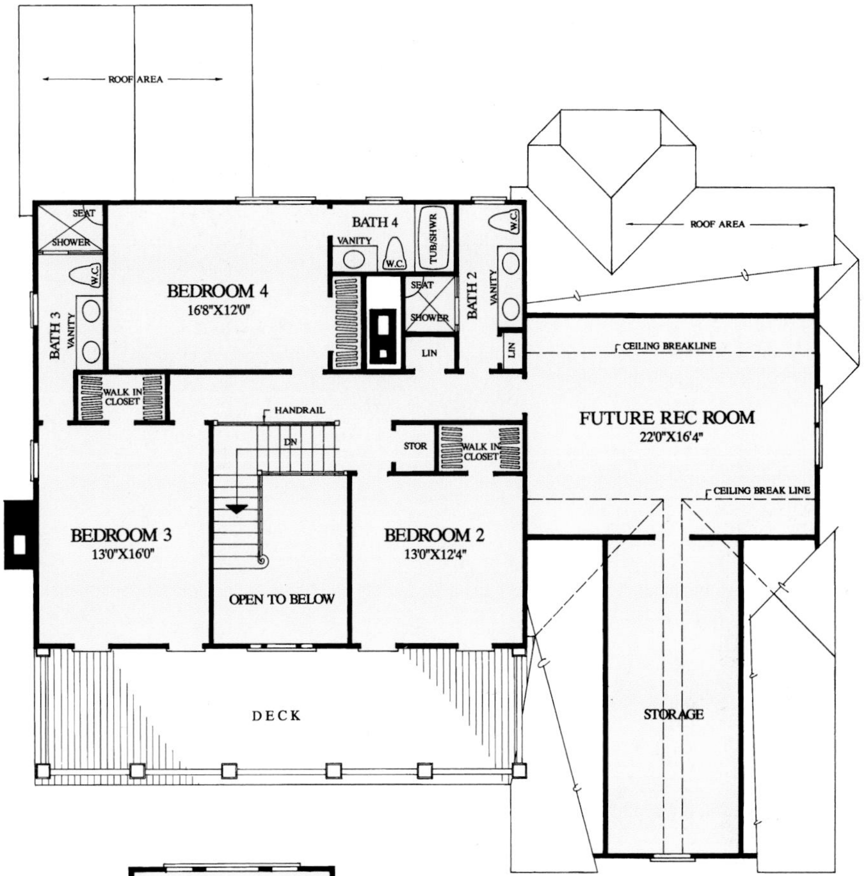
ROOF AREA
BEDROOM 4
16'8"X12'0"
BATH 4
VANITY
W.C.
TUB/SHWR
SEAT
SHOWER
LIN
BATH 2
VANITY
W.C.
LIN
BATH 3
VANITY
W.C.
SEAT
SHOWER
WALK IN CLOSET
HANDRAIL
DN
STOR
WALK IN CLOSET
ROOF AREA
CEILING BREAKLINE
FUTURE REC ROOM
22'0"X16'4"
CEILING BREAK LINE
BEDROOM 3
13'0"X16'0"
OPEN TO BELOW
BEDROOM 2
13'0"X12'4"
DECK
STORAGE

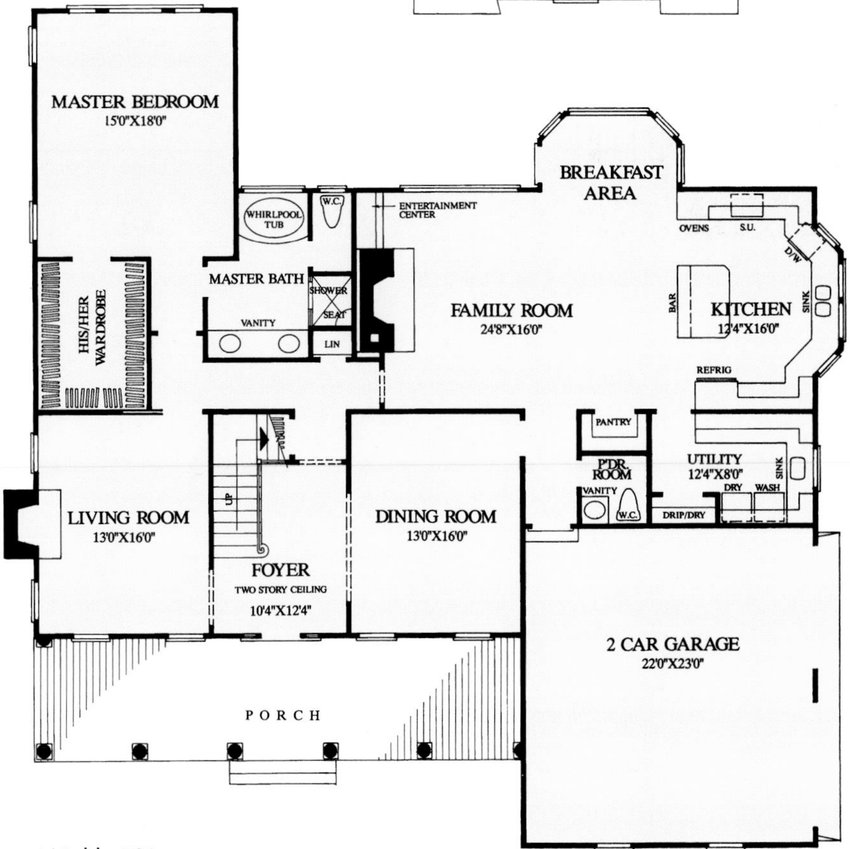
MASTER BEDROOM
15'0"X18'0"
BREAKFAST AREA
WHIRLPOOL TUB
W.C.
ENTERTAINMENT CENTER
OVENS
S.U.
D/W
MASTER BATH
SHOWER
SEAT
VANITY
LIN
HIS/HER WARDROBE
FAMILY ROOM
24'8"X16'0"
BAR
KITCHEN
12'4"X16'0"
SINK
REFRIG
PANTRY
PDR. ROOM
VANITY
W.C.
UTILITY
12'4"X8'0"
SINK
DRY
WASH
DRIP/DRY
UP
LIVING ROOM
13'0"X16'0"
FOYER
TWO STORY CEILING
10'4"X12'4"
DINING ROOM
13'0"X16'0"
2 CAR GARAGE
22'0"X23'0"
PORCH

Main Level: 2,086 square feet
Upper Level: 1,094 square feet
Total: 3,180 square feet
Future Recreation Room:
372 square feet
Optional basement plan is included

Width 62'
Depth 61'-10"

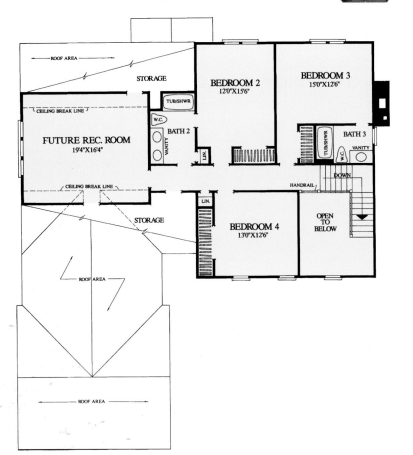

ROOF AREA

STORAGE

CEILING BREAK LINE

TUB/SHWR

FUTURE REC. ROOM
19'4"X16'4"

W.C.

BATH 2

VANITY

BEDROOM 2
12'0"X15'6"

BEDROOM 3
15'0"X12'6"

LIN.

TUB/SHWR

W.C.

BATH 3

VANITY

CEILING BREAK LINE

STORAGE

LIN.

BEDROOM 4
13'0"X12'6"

HANDRAIL

DOWN

OPEN TO BELOW

ROOF AREA

ROOF AREA

Main Level: 2,307 square feet
Upper Level: 926 square feet
Total: 3,233 square feet
Future Recreation Room:
  334 square feet
Optional basement plan is included

BREAKFAST AREA
12'0"X9'0"

BAR

SINK

D/W

KITCHEN
12'0"X12'8"

RANGE

REFG.

PANTRY

MASTER BEDROOM
17'0"X15'0"

FAMILY ROOM
24'8"X20'0"

BOOKCASE

SEAT

SHWR

VANITY

LINEN

MASTER BATH

WHIRLPOOL TUB

W.C.

SHLV

SHLV

HIS/HER WARDROBE

WASH   DRY

DR/P? DRY

UTILITY
7'0"X11'0"

LIN.

STOR.

PDR ROOM

VANITY

W.C.

DINING ROOM
15'6"X12'6"

UP

FOYER
TWO STORY CEILING
11'6"X12'6"

LIVING ROOM
13'0"X20'8"

STORAGE

STOOP

2 CAR GARAGE
23'4"X21'8"

Width 69'-4"
Depth 65'

Cape Charles—Design Q139

What poise. What grace. What crisp, precise detail. What a stirring of nostalgic feelings upon seeing The Cape Charles just beyond—sitting regally but gracefully, shimmering at the water's edge. The proportions, the cedar shingles in the gabled ends, the chimney configuration—all this and more awaken dreams of "home" and all that it encompasses. Dreams really do come true—yours can too!

The Essence of Southern Style

*C*atering to a lifestyle filled with richness and grace, the historic homes of the South were, and are, true showpieces. These homes, as represented in The Essence of Southern Style, are grand and glorious, with some resembling their contemporary counterpart—the prairie farmhouse—dressed up with wide porches and dormered windows. Porch columns are often round, reminiscent of Southern Georgians or columned Southern Colonials.

The Shenandoah II (page 102) is an example of this famous farmhouse style. A covered porch, handsomely supported by columns and enhanced with dormered windows, coaxes gentle breezes and the fragrant bouquet of magnolias and dogwood blossoms inside, filling the house with nature's sweet aroma.

Tailor-made to suit the legendary Butlers, The Savannah (page 114) provides a true Southern classic. Imagine it surrounded by Live Oaks draped in silvery Spanish moss. The exterior provides as dramatic a backdrop for today's coming-out parties and weddings as it did for yesterday's Southern belles.

Reflective of the raised cottages typical of the Southern coastal plains, The Currituck Cottage (page 126) has all the ingredients that evoke the nostalgic feeling of "coming home." Start with a dash of lattice on the lower or raised level; add a splash of color, compliments of wooden shutters decorating the windows; and mix in a wrapping porch for good measure and you have a blue-ribbon winner.

The plans offered in this chapter are apt reminders of America's architectural heritage. Each design represents the gracious expression of Southern style. Together they provide a grand collection of homes for refined living.

The Natchez II—Design Q140

The Briars in Natchez, Mississippi—one of the most sophisticated examples of the planter's cottage architecture of the lower Mississippi valley. From the Briars evolved the Natchez II. Jefferson Davis married Varina Howell in the Briars' parlor and one may still visit this beautifully preserved site today. The Natchez II strikes a universal cord—inducing many fortunate individuals and families to call it "home".

Main Level: 2,648 square feet
Upper Level: 1,253 square feet
Total: 3,901 square feet
Future Recreation Room:
 540 square feet
Future Bedroom 5: 355 square feet

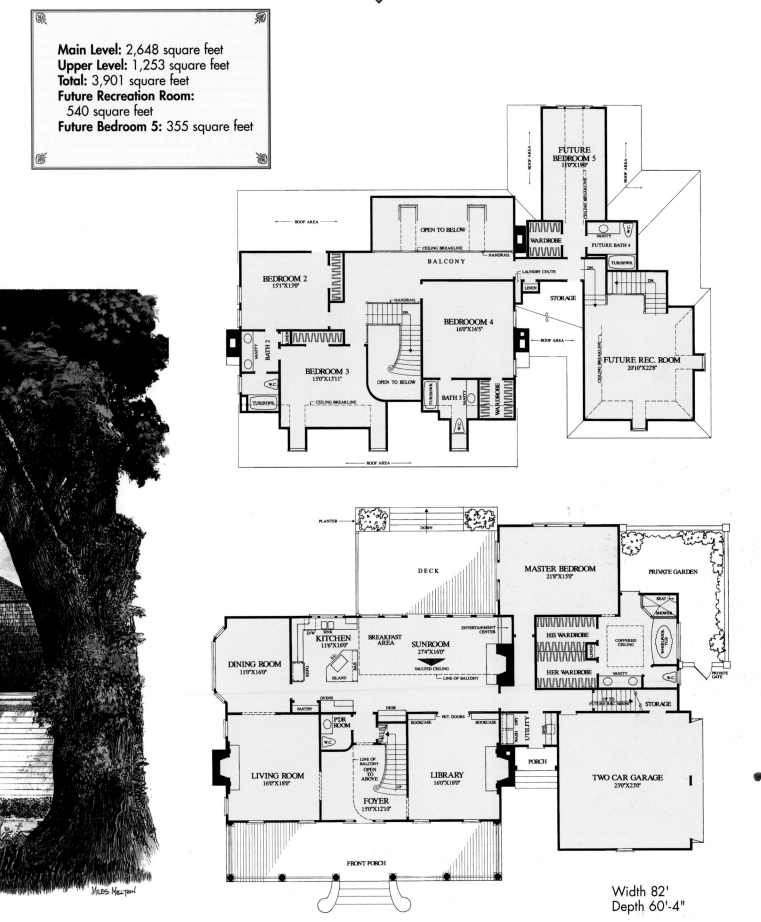

Width 82'
Depth 60'-4"

Somerset—Design Q141

As a child she made up stories. Summers were spent gazing at the sky, creating cloud pictures and stories to go with them. The wind presented an everchanging canvas, transforming the billowing clouds from one image to another. The stories penned in her child-scrawl were packed away, but as a young woman, she never lost her dream of becoming an author. Today, she lingers over a cup of tea in the breakfast room, her mind developing the plot for her latest novel. Dreams do come true in The Somerset—her home.

Square Footage: 2,394

Width 82'-6"
Depth 52'-8"

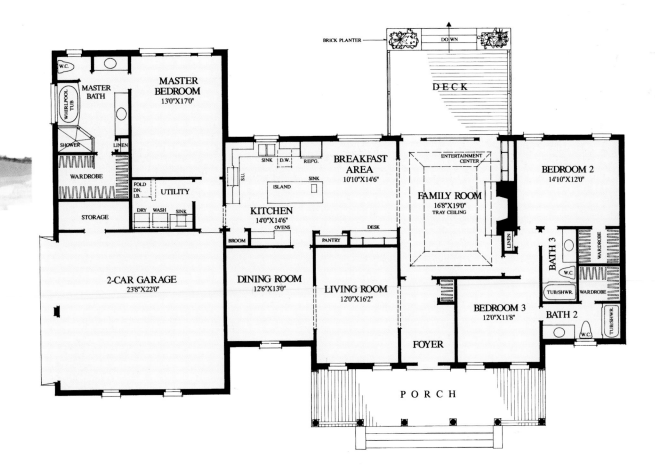

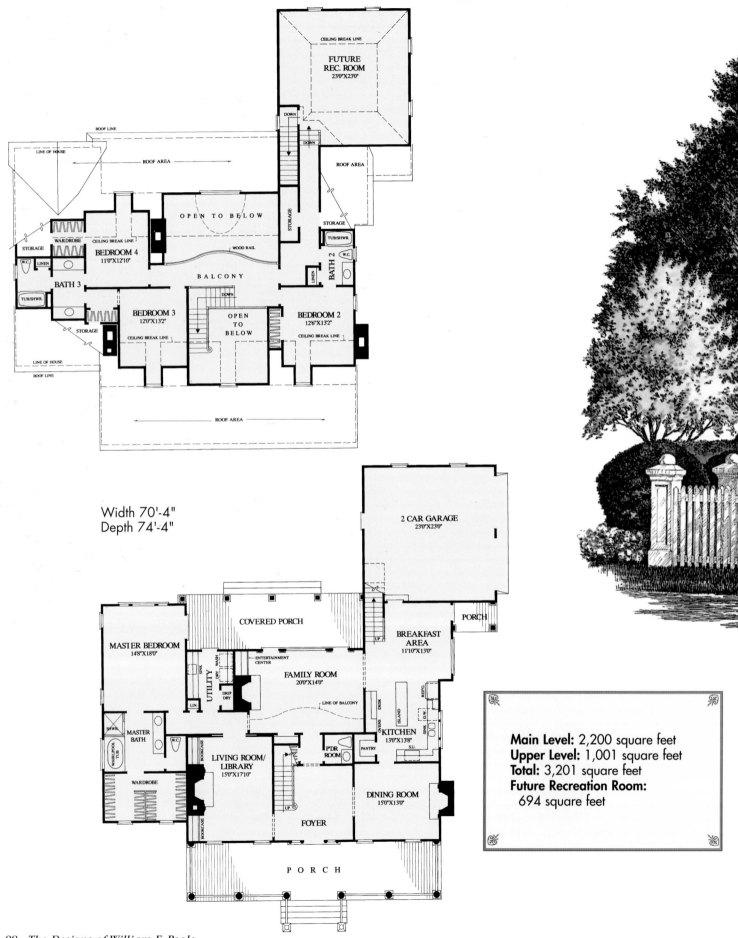

FUTURE
REC. ROOM
23'0"X23'0"

BEDROOM 4
11'0"X12'10"

BATH 3

BEDROOM 3
12'0"X13'2"

OPEN
TO
BELOW

BALCONY

BEDROOM 2
12'6"X13'2"

BATH 2

OPEN TO BELOW

Width 70'-4"
Depth 74'-4"

2 CAR GARAGE
23'0"X23'0"

PORCH

COVERED PORCH

MASTER BEDROOM
14'8"X18'0"

UTILITY

FAMILY ROOM
20'0"X14'0"

BREAKFAST
AREA
11'10"X13'0"

MASTER
BATH

KITCHEN
13'0"X13'8"

LIVING ROOM/
LIBRARY
15'0"X17'10"

P'DR
ROOM

PANTRY

FOYER

DINING ROOM
15'0"X13'0"

PORCH

Main Level: 2,200 square feet
Upper Level: 1,001 square feet
Total: 3,201 square feet
Future Recreation Room:
694 square feet

Melrose — Design Q142

Porch swings, trailing wisteria vines, crocus that look like Easter eggs, buttercups and chirping birds—all senses are invaded with memories of our childhood. Visits to grandma's home included stories told, stories heard, and stories embellished upon. The best possible gift—here we were taught the lessons it had taken our grandparents a lifetime to learn. All this beauty, and a legacy too, was set in the old South—and in the Melrose.

Turnberry—Design Q143

Aunt Harriet lived in a home much like The Turnberry. She wore wide brimmed, flowered hats and never went calling without first donning her white cotton gloves. But every day of her life was an adventure. While watching a well-known comedy, my cousin B.J. and I—between fits of laughter—agreed the leading lady fit Aunt Harriet right down to her familiar white gloves. As time marches on, this home's unique character will continue on and on—delightful, timeless. Like Aunt Harriet.

MILES MELTON

Main Level: 1,634 square feet
Upper Level: 619 square feet
Total: 2,253 square feet
Future Recreation Room:
  229 square feet

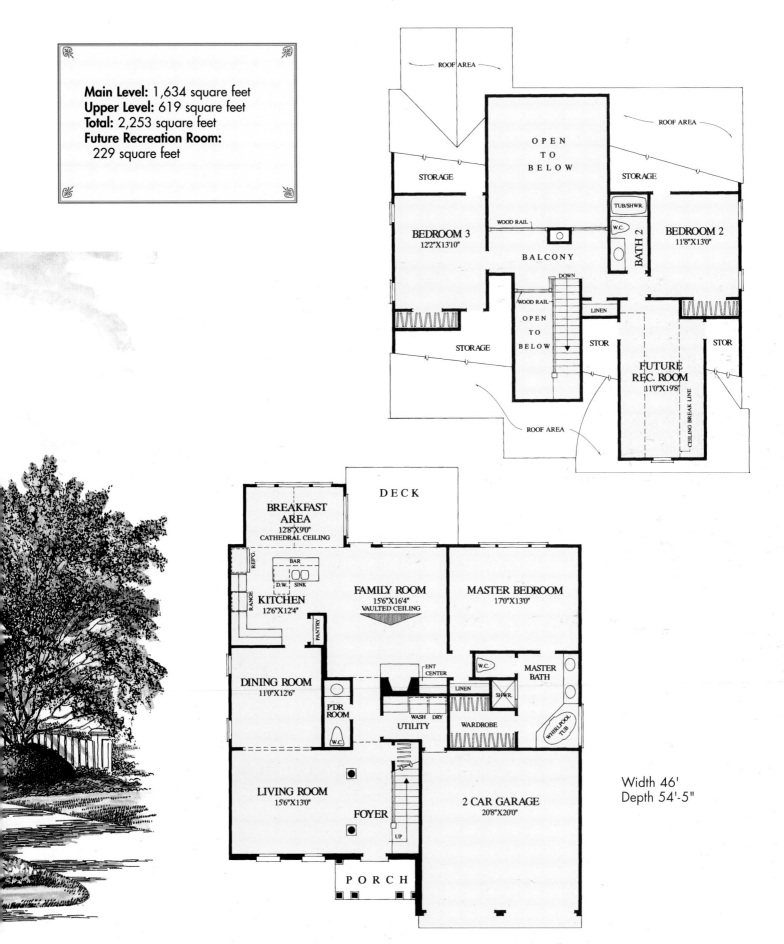

ROOF AREA

ROOF AREA

OPEN
TO
BELOW

STORAGE

STORAGE

WOOD RAIL

TUB/SHWR.

W.C.

BEDROOM 3
12'2"X13'10"

BEDROOM 2
11'8"X13'0"

BATH 2

BALCONY

DOWN

WOOD RAIL

LINEN

OPEN
TO
BELOW

STORAGE

STOR

STOR

FUTURE
REC. ROOM
11'0"X19'8"

CEILING BREAK LINE

ROOF AREA

DECK

BREAKFAST
AREA
12'8"X9'0"
CATHEDRAL CEILING

REFG.

BAR

D.W. SINK

RANGE

KITCHEN
12'6"X12'4"

PANTRY

FAMILY ROOM
15'6"X16'4"
VAULTED CEILING

MASTER BEDROOM
17'0"X13'0"

ENT
CENTER

W.C.

MASTER
BATH

DINING ROOM
11'0"X12'6"

P'DR
ROOM

LINEN

SHWR.

W.C.

WASH DRY

WARDROBE

WHIRLPOOL
TUB

UTILITY

LIVING ROOM
15'6"X13'0"

FOYER

2 CAR GARAGE
20'8"X20'0"

UP

Width 46'
Depth 54'-5"

PORCH

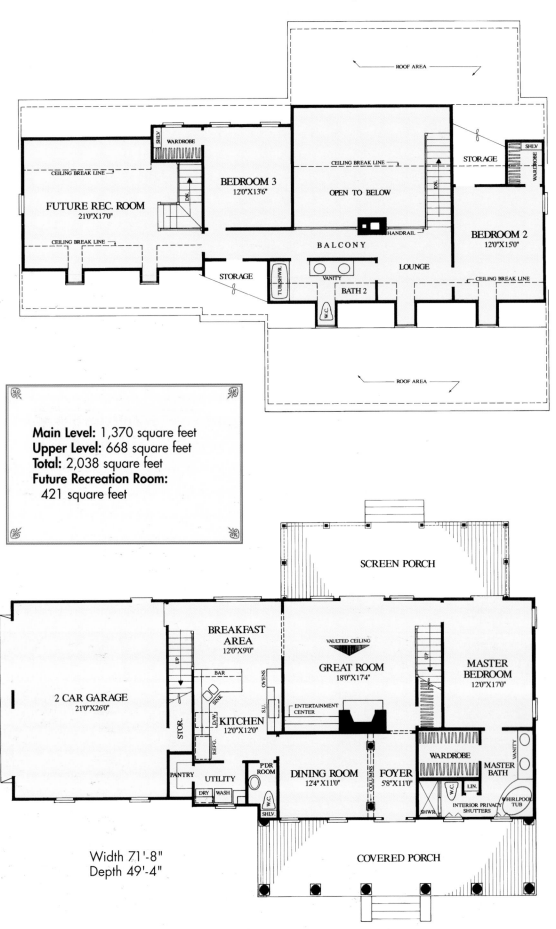

ROOF AREA

SHLV
WARDROBE

CEILING BREAK LINE

FUTURE REC. ROOM
21'0"X17'0"

BEDROOM 3
12'0"X13'6"

CEILING BREAK LINE

OPEN TO BELOW

STORAGE

SHLV
WARDROBE

DN

CEILING BREAK LINE

CEILING BREAK LINE

HANDRAIL

BALCONY

BEDROOM 2
12'0"X15'0"

STORAGE

TUB&SHWR

VANITY

LOUNGE

CEILING BREAK LINE

BATH 2

W.C.

ROOF AREA

Main Level: 1,370 square feet
Upper Level: 668 square feet
Total: 2,038 square feet
Future Recreation Room:
   421 square feet

SCREEN PORCH

BREAKFAST
AREA
12'0"X9'0"

BAR

VAULTED CEILING

GREAT ROOM
18'0"X17'4"

UP

MASTER
BEDROOM
12'0"X17'0"

2 CAR GARAGE
21'0"X26'0"

UP

STOR.

SINK

D/W

KITCHEN
12'0"X12'0"

REFG.

OVENS

S.U.

ENTERTAINMENT
CENTER

WARDROBE

VANITY

PANTRY

UTILITY

P'DR
ROOM

DINING ROOM
12'4"X11'0"

FOYER
5'8"X11'0"

MASTER
BATH

DRY

WASH

W.C.

SHLV

COLUMNS

W.C.

LIN.

SHWR

INTERIOR PRIVACY
SHUTTERS

WHIRLPOOL
TUB

Width 71'-8"
Depth 49'-4"

COVERED PORCH

Shenandoah II—Design Q144

The shenandoah II is a home built for celebrations. They began the day our family moved into this wonderful home and continue through the years. The crisp air of autumn finds a line-up of smiling Jack-O-lanterns and soon it will be time to wind the stately columns with twinkling lights that brighten the snowy, silent nights. In a blink of an eye, the first signs of spring provide a colorful backdrop for hidden Easter eggs. And on the 4th of July, the Stars and Stripes will proudly wave. At Shenandoah II each day is a celebration of home and family. May the celebrations live on—here's to a wonderful life!

The La Petite Natchez—Design Q145

It is often said that good things come in small packages—ask any connoisseur of fine jewelry! You made a request and we listened, thus from The Natchez sprang The La Petite Natchez. Without sacrificing any of the rooms or amenities of the original, The Natchez was proportionately reduced and The La Petite Natchez was born. This generation will create the history for the La Petite. May it be a gracious time!

Upper Level floor plan:
- STORAGE
- ROOF AREA
- OPEN TO SUNROOM BELOW
- STORAGE
- LINE OF HOUSE
- ROOF AREA
- BEDROOM 4 13'10"X12'0"
- BALCONY
- WOOD RAIL
- LAUNDRY CHUTE
- STORAGE
- DOWN
- DOWN
- WOOD RAIL
- DOWN
- BATH 3
- WOOD RAIL
- LIN.
- BEDROOM 2 14'0"X13'4"
- STORAGE
- CEILING BREAK LINE
- FUT. REC. ROOM 19'0"X21'0"
- W.C.
- BEDROOM 3 14'6"X12'0"
- OPEN TO FOYER BELOW
- TUB/SHWR
- WARDROBE
- TUB/SHWR.
- BATH 2
- CEILING BREAK LINE
- LINE OF HOUSE
- W.C.
- SHELF
- ROOF AREA
- LINE OF HOUSE

Main Level: 2,092 square feet
Upper Level: 1,045 square feet
Total: 3,137 square feet
Future Recreation Room:
  546 square feet

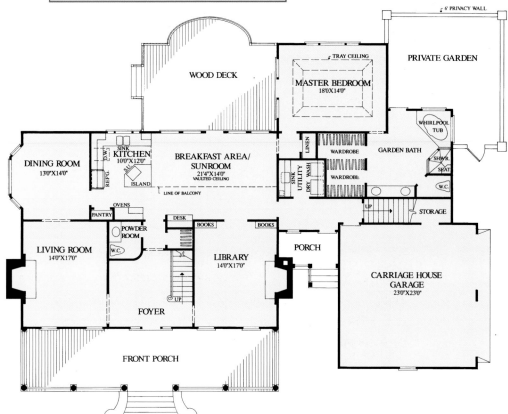

Main Level floor plan:
- WOOD DECK
- TRAY CEILING
- MASTER BEDROOM 18'0"X14'0"
- PRIVATE GARDEN
- 6' PRIVACY WALL
- DINING ROOM 13'0"X14'0"
- SINK
- D.W.
- KITCHEN 10'0"X12'0"
- REFG.
- ISLAND
- BREAKFAST AREA/ SUNROOM 21'4"X14'0" VAULTED CEILING
- LINE OF BALCONY
- LINEN
- WARDROBE
- SINK
- UTILITY
- WASH
- DRY
- WARDROBE
- GARDEN BATH
- WHIRLPOOL TUB
- SHWR. SEAT
- W.C.
- OVENS
- PANTRY
- DESK
- BOOKS
- BOOKS
- UP
- STORAGE
- POWDER ROOM
- W.C.
- LIVING ROOM 14'0"X17'0"
- LIBRARY 14'0"X17'0"
- PORCH
- FOYER
- UP
- CARRIAGE HOUSE GARAGE 23'0"X23'0"
- FRONT PORCH

Width 77'
Depth 56'-4"

Main Level: 2,320 square feet
Upper Level: 1,057 square feet
Total: 3,377 square feet
Future Recreation Room:
  608 square feet

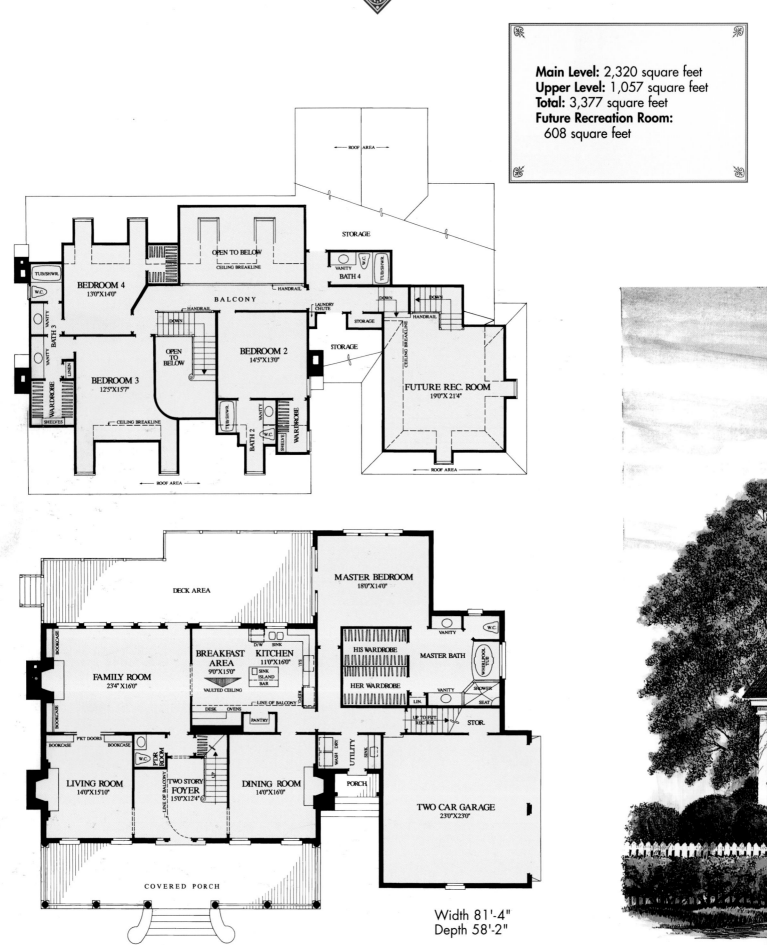

ROOF AREA

STORAGE

OPEN TO BELOW
CEILING BREAKLINE

BATH 4

VANITY W.C. TUB/SHWR.

TUB/SHWR.
W.C.

BEDROOM 4
13'0"X14'0"

VANITY BATH 3 VANITY

HANDRAIL

BALCONY

DOWN DOWN

HANDRAIL

STORAGE

DOWN HANDRAIL

OPEN
TO
BELOW

BEDROOM 2
14'5"X13'0"

STORAGE

CEILING BREAKLINE

WARDROBE

LINEN

BEDROOM 3
12'5"X15'7"

FUTURE REC. ROOM
19'0"X 21'4"

SHELVES

CEILING BREAKLINE

TUB/SHWR.

VANITY

BATH 2

W.C.

SHELVES WARDROBE

ROOF AREA

ROOF AREA

DECK AREA

MASTER BEDROOM
18'0"X14'0"

BOOKCASE

FAMILY ROOM
23'4"X16'0"

BREAKFAST
AREA
9'0"X15'0"

KITCHEN
11'0"X16'0"

D/W SINK

HIS WARDROBE

VANITY

W.C.

MASTER BATH

VAULTED CEILING

SINK
ISLAND
BAR

HER WARDROBE

WHIRLPOOL
TUB

SHOWER

BOOKCASE

DESK OVENS

LINE OF BALCONY

REF/FZ

LIN.

VANITY

SEAT

PANTRY

UP TO FUT
REC. RM.

STOR.

PKT DOORS

BOOKCASE BOOKCASE

W.C.

PDR.
ROOM

WASH DRY

UTILITY

SINK

LINE OF BALCONY

LIVING ROOM
14'0"X15'10"

TWO STORY
FOYER
15'0"X12'4"

UP

DINING ROOM
14'0"X16'0"

PORCH

TWO CAR GARAGE
23'0"X23'0"

COVERED PORCH

Width 81'-4"
Depth 58'-2"

Camellia Cottage II—Design Q146

*T*he struggle to return home. A young girl stands with a wicker basket over one arm while clutching her small dog in the other. She closes her eyes, clicks together the heels of her ruby-red slippers and utters repeatedly, "There's no place like home." Dorothy, and a multitude of others have touched our hearts and souls with their determination to reach their homes and families. Home. It's more that just a place to live. The Camellia Cottage II is dedicated to the wonderful characters, fictional and non-fictional, that believe home is an essential part of their beings.

Sunnyside—Design Q147

Fine china and milk-laced tea, melt-in-your-mouth shortbread cookies and cocoa-dusted meringues—for two little girls dressed in their Sunday best—this was the epitome of elegance. Our weekly afternoon tea with Grammie was a ritual never missed. Sunnyside—her tidewater Virginian farmhouse—is a quietly elegant home with a warm, welcoming porch that invites tea parties and other lasting traditions.

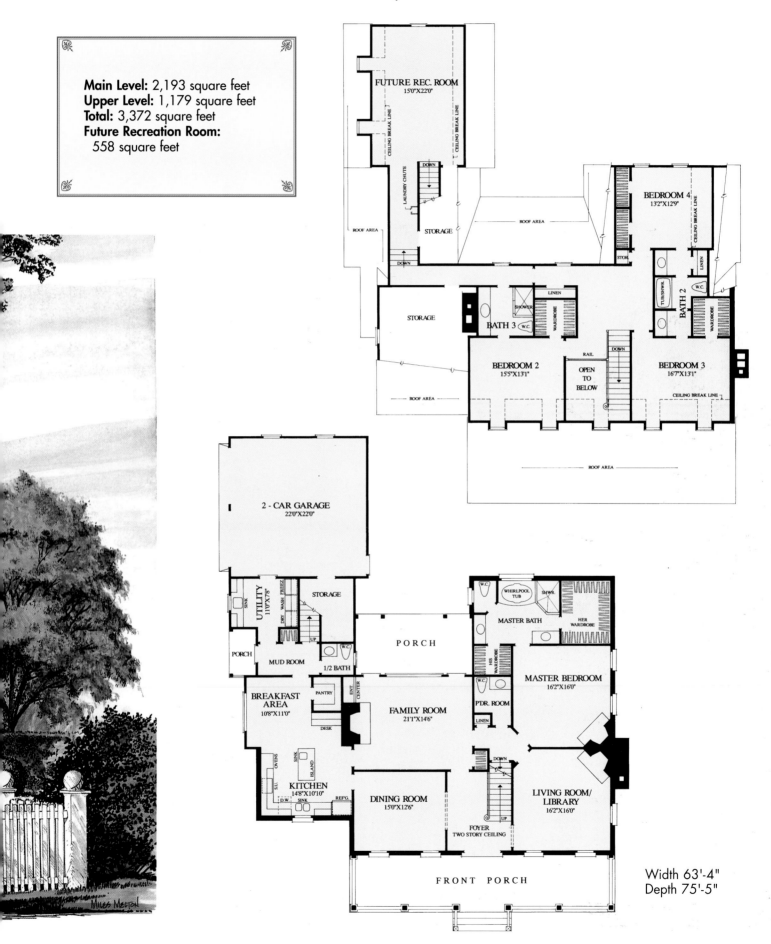

Main Level: 2,193 square feet
Upper Level: 1,179 square feet
Total: 3,372 square feet
Future Recreation Room:
 558 square feet

FUTURE REC. ROOM
15'0"X22'0"

CEILING BREAK LINE

LAUNDRY CHUTE

DOWN

STORAGE

ROOF AREA

ROOF AREA

DOWN

STORAGE

BEDROOM 4
13'2"X12'9"

CEILING BREAK LINE

LINEN

STOR.

TUB/SHWR.

BATH 2

W.C.

WARDROBE

LINEN

SHOWER

BATH 3

W.C.

WARDROBE

BEDROOM 2
15'5"X13'1"

RAIL

OPEN
TO
BELOW

DOWN

BEDROOM 3
16'7"X13'1"

CEILING BREAK LINE

ROOF AREA

ROOF AREA

2 - CAR GARAGE
22'0"X22'0"

UTILITY
11'0"X7'8"

SINK

DRY WASH FREEZ

STORAGE

W.C.

WHIRLPOOL
TUB

SHWR.

MASTER BATH

HER
WARDROBE

UP

PORCH

PORCH

MUD ROOM

1/2 BATH

W.C.

ENT. CENTER

HIS
WARDROBE

W.C.

MASTER BEDROOM
16'2"X16'0"

BREAKFAST
AREA
10'8"X11'0"

PANTRY

DESK

FAMILY ROOM
21'1"X14'6"

PDR. ROOM

LINEN

OVENS

SINK

ISLAND

KITCHEN
14'8"X10'10"

D.W. SINK

REFG.

DINING ROOM
15'0"X12'6"

FOYER
TWO STORY CEILING

DOWN

UP

LIVING ROOM/
LIBRARY
16'2"X16'0"

FRONT PORCH

Width 63'-4"
Depth 75'-5"

Belle Grove—Design Q148

An inviting home, the Belle Grove, bespeaks magnolias, dogwood blossoms, butterflies and the peaceful hospitality of the gracious South. Its inspiration came from Cottage Gardens. A noteworthy feature, the rare combination of the Natchez gallery recessed beneath an unbroken slope of gable roof with a triangular pediment. This home takes its que from the gracious formality indigenous to the typical Mississippi River Delta Planters' Cottage.

Main Level: 2,000 square feet
Upper Level: 1,062 square feet
Total: 3,062 square feet
Future Recreation Room:
  683 square feet

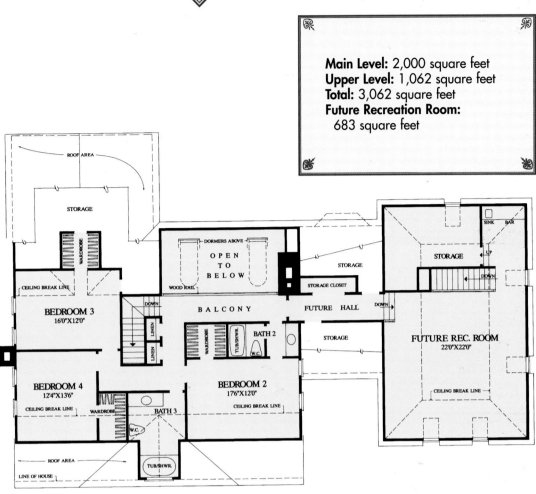

ROOF AREA

STORAGE

DORMERS ABOVE

OPEN
TO
BELOW

WOOD RAIL

STORAGE

STORAGE CLOSET

SINK   BAR

STORAGE

UP

DOWN

CEILING BREAK LINE

WARDROBE

BEDROOM 3
16'0"X12'0"

DOWN

LINEN

LINEN

BALCONY

FUTURE   HALL

DOWN

STORAGE

FUTURE REC. ROOM
22'0"X22'0"

WARDROBE

TUB/SHWR.

BATH 2

W.C.

BEDROOM 4
12'4"X13'6"

BEDROOM 2
17'6"X12'0"

CEILING BREAK LINE

CEILING BREAK LINE

WARDROBE

CEILING BREAK LINE

BATH 3

W.C.

ROOF AREA

TUB/SHWR.

LINE OF HOUSE

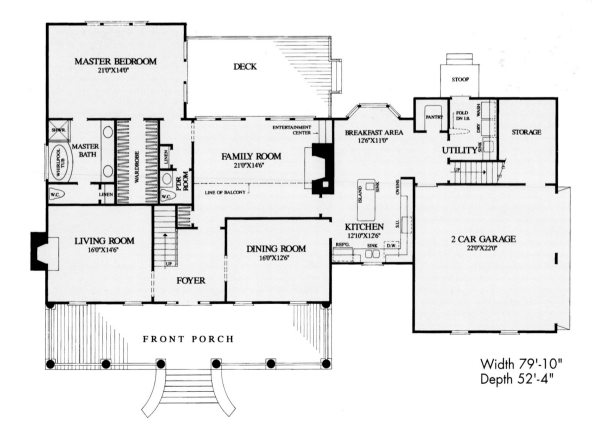

MASTER BEDROOM
21'0"X14'0"

DECK

STOOP

SHWR.

MASTER
BATH

WHIRLPOOL
TUB

WARDROBE

LINEN

PDR
ROOM

ENTERTAINMENT
CENTER

BREAKFAST AREA
12'6"X11'0"

PANTRY

FOLD
DN I.B.

WASH

DRY

STORAGE

UTILITY

SINK

W.C.

LINEN

W.C.

FAMILY ROOM
21'0"X14'6"

LINE OF BALCONY

ISLAND

SINK

OVENS

UP

LIVING ROOM
16'0"X14'6"

UP

FOYER

DINING ROOM
16'0"X12'6"

KITCHEN
12'10"X12'6"

REF'G.

SINK

D.W.

2 CAR GARAGE
22'0"X22'0"

FRONT PORCH

Width 79'-10"
Depth 52'-4"

Mount Aire II—Design Q149

Parasols, high-necked lace collars, white gloves and gold-tipped canes adorned lovely ladies from the past as they sipped their tea and visited amid the roses, hydrangeas, tulips and day lilies. The Mount Aire II, like many antebellum homes that capture the romance of the old South, graciously reflects the Greek Revival style of architecture. A home that is...simply Southern at its best!

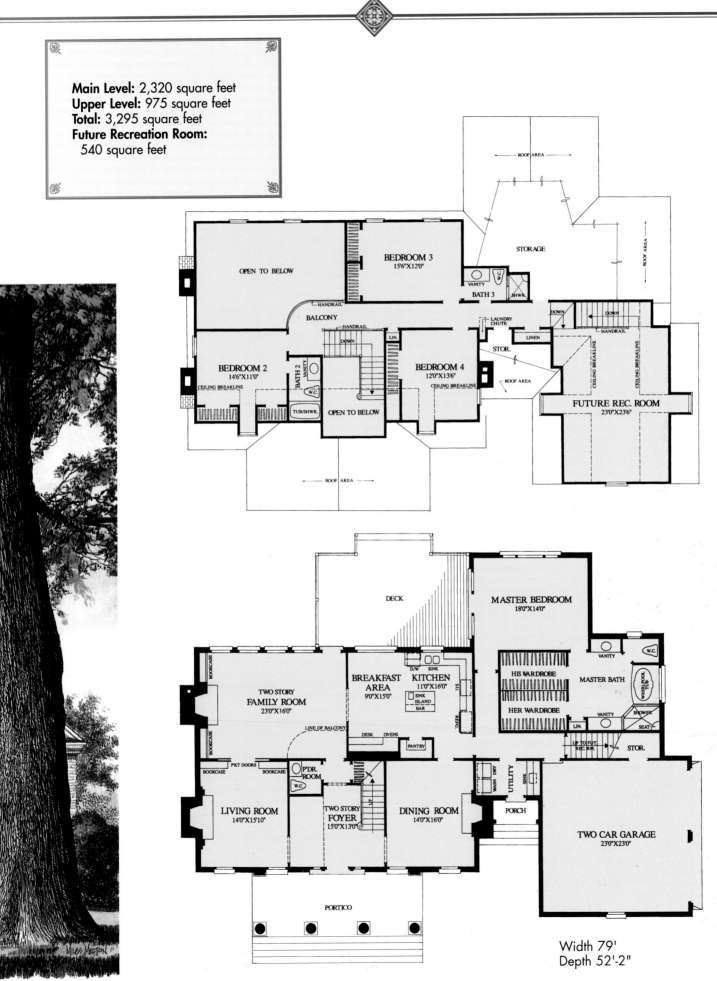

Main Level: 2,320 square feet
Upper Level: 975 square feet
Total: 3,295 square feet
Future Recreation Room:
   540 square feet

ROOF AREA

STORAGE

BEDROOM 3
15'6"X12'0"

OPEN TO BELOW

VANITY
W.C.
BATH 3
SHWR.

ROOF AREA

HANDRAIL
BALCONY

HANDRAIL
DOWN
LAUNDRY CHUTE
DOWN
DOWN
HANDRAIL
LIN.
LINEN

BEDROOM 2
14'6"X11'0"

VANITY
BATH 2
W.C.
CEILING BREAKLINE
TUB/SHWR.

DOWN

BEDROOM 4
12'0"X13'6"

STOR.

ROOF AREA

CEILING BREAKLINE

OPEN TO BELOW

CEILING BREAKLINE

CEILING BREAKLINE

FUTURE REC. ROOM
23'0"X23'6"

ROOF AREA

DECK

MASTER BEDROOM
18'0"X14'0"

VANITY
W.C.

BOOKCASE

TWO STORY
FAMILY ROOM
23'0"X16'0"

BREAKFAST
AREA
9'0"X15'0"

D/W   SINK

KITCHEN
11'0"X16'0"

S.L.

SINK
ISLAND
BAR

REFG.

HIS WARDROBE

MASTER BATH

WHIRLPOOL
TUB

BOOKCASE

HER WARDROBE

LIN.

VANITY

SHOWER
SEAT

LINE OF BALCONY

DESK   OVENS

PANTRY

UP TO FUT.
REC. RM.

STOR.

BOOKCASE

PKT DOORS

BOOKCASE

P'DR.
ROOM
W.C.

BOOKCASE

LIVING ROOM
14'0"X15'10"

TWO STORY
FOYER
15'0"X13'0"

UP

DINING ROOM
14'0"X16'0"

WASH DRY

UTILITY

SINK

PORCH

TWO CAR GARAGE
23'0"X23'0"

PORTICO

Width 79'
Depth 52'-2"

The Savannah—Design Q150

Can you hear it? It's the soft rustle of crinolines beneath the fashionable watered-silk gowns of the county's young Southern belles. As they sashay through the grand entrance of The Savannah their thoughts turn to the forthcoming festivities. Back-yard barbecues held at this stately home are often weekend events that hold a wealth of possibilities. Peeking past the rim of her parasol, she smiles a coy smile—the gentleman with the rogue's reputation from Charleston is making his way toward her. The genteel, Southern way of life is alive at The Savannah.

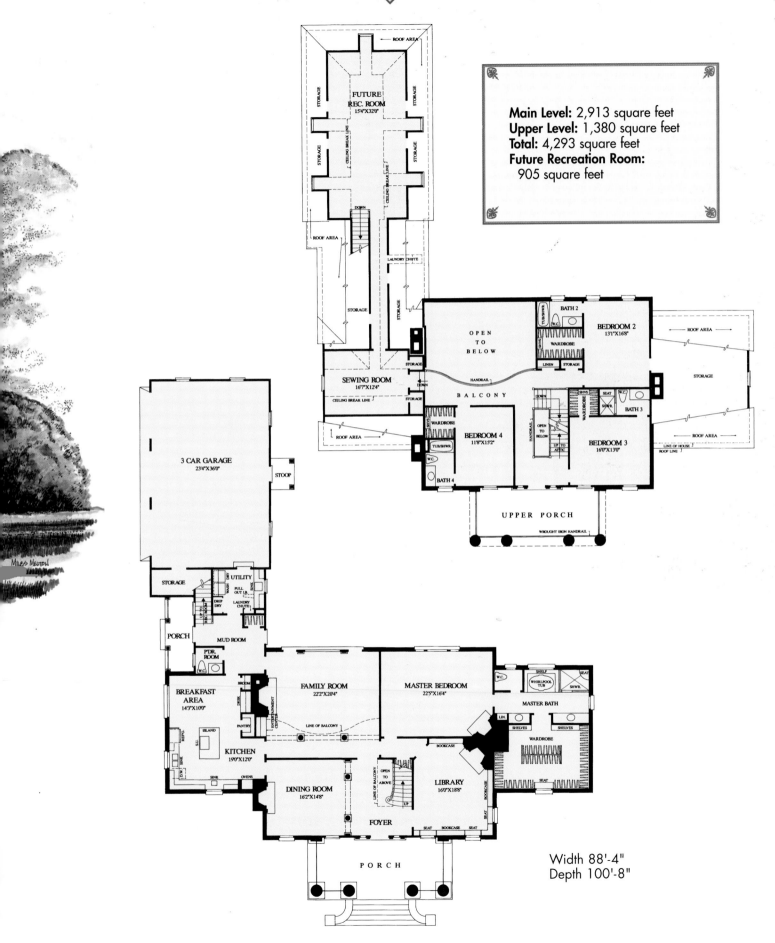

FUTURE
REC. ROOM
15'4"X32'0"

STORAGE

ROOF AREA

CEILING BREAK LINE

DOWN

ROOF AREA

STORAGE

LAUNDRY CHUTE

STORAGE

STORAGE

Main Level: 2,913 square feet
Upper Level: 1,380 square feet
Total: 4,293 square feet
Future Recreation Room:
905 square feet

BATH 2

OPEN
TO
BELOW

WARDROBE

BEDROOM 2
13'1"X16'8"

ROOF AREA

STORAGE

LINEN   STORAGE

HANDRAIL

SEWING ROOM
16'7"X12'4"

BALCONY

STORAGE

SEAT   W.C.

DOWN

CEILING BREAK LINE

STORAGE

WARDROBE

DOWN

OPEN
TO
BELOW

BATH 3

3 CAR GARAGE
23'4"X36'0"

WARDROBE

BEDROOM 4
11'8"X15'2"

HANDRAIL

UP TO
ATTIC

BEDROOM 3
16'0"X13'0"

ROOF AREA

STOOP

ROOF AREA

LINE OF HOUSE
ROOF LINE

TUB/SHWR.

W.C.

BATH 4

STORAGE

UP
REC.
ROOM

UTILITY

WASH   DRY

PULL
OUT LDR.

SINK

UPPER PORCH

WROUGHT IRON HANDRAIL

PORCH

DRIP
DRY

LAUNDRY
CHUTE

MUD ROOM

PDR.
ROOM

W.C.

BREAKFAST
AREA
14'3"X10'0"

BROOM

DESK

PANTRY

FAMILY ROOM
22'2"X20'4"

ENTERTAINMENT CENTER

MASTER BEDROOM
22'5"X16'4"

W.C.

SHELF

WHIRLPOOL
TUB

SEAT

SHWR.

MASTER BATH

ISLAND

KITCHEN
19'0"X12'0"

LINE OF BALCONY

REFRIG.

LIN

SHELVES

SHELVES

BOOKCASE

WARDROBE

SINK

D.W.

SINK   OVENS

DINING ROOM
16'2"X14'8"

LINE OF BALCONY

OPEN
TO
ABOVE

UP

LIBRARY
16'0"X18'8"

BOOKCASE

SEAT

SEAT

FOYER

SEAT   BOOKCASE   SEAT

PORCH

Width 88'-4"
Depth 100'-8"

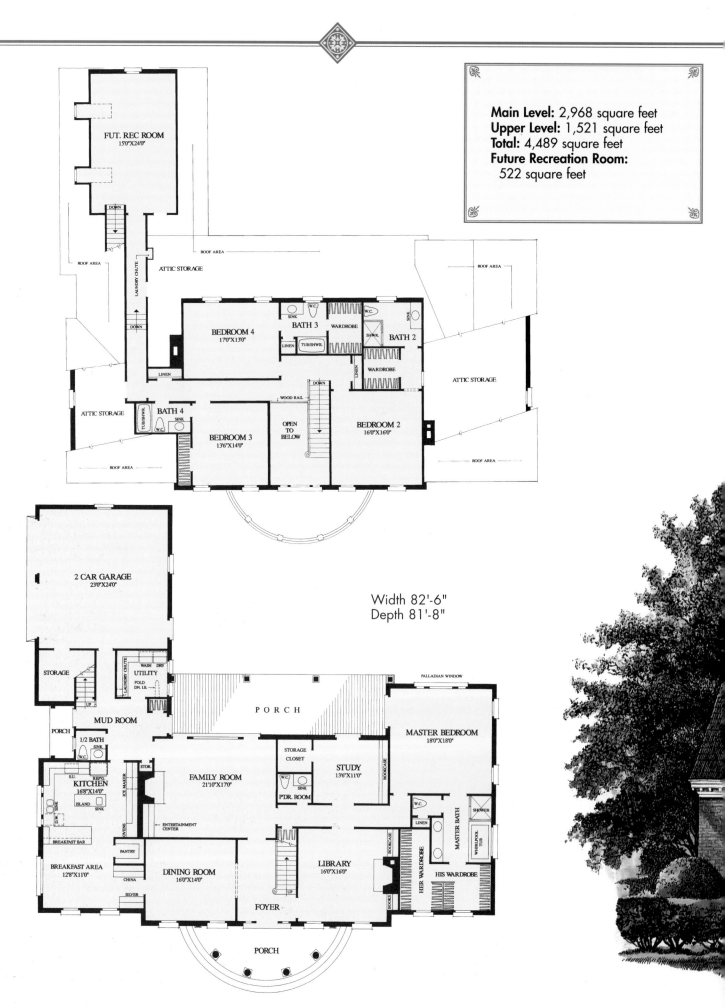

FUT. REC ROOM
15'0"X24'0"

ROOF AREA

ATTIC STORAGE

LAUNDRY CHUTE

DOWN

ROOF AREA

DOWN

BEDROOM 4
17'0"X13'0"

BATH 3

W.C.
SINK
WARDROBE

W.C.
SHWR.
BATH 2
SINK

LINEN
TUB/SHWR.

WARDROBE

ROOF AREA

ATTIC STORAGE

LINEN

LINEN

ATTIC STORAGE

WOOD RAIL

DOWN

BATH 4
TUB/SHWR.
W.C.
SINK

BEDROOM 3
13'6"X14'0"

OPEN TO BELOW

BEDROOM 2
16'0"X16'0"

ROOF AREA

ROOF AREA

Main Level: 2,968 square feet
Upper Level: 1,521 square feet
Total: 4,489 square feet
Future Recreation Room:
522 square feet

2 CAR GARAGE
23'0"X24'0"

Width 82'-6"
Depth 81'-8"

STORAGE

LAUNDRY CHUTE
UTILITY
FOLD DN. LD.
WASH DRY

UP

PORCH

MUD ROOM

PALLADIAN WINDOW

PORCH

1/2 BATH
SINK
W.C.

SU.
REFG.
ICE MAKER

KITCHEN
16'8"X14'0"
ISLAND
SINK

FAMILY ROOM
21'10"X17'0"

ENTERTAINMENT CENTER

STORAGE
CLOSET

W.C.
SINK
P'DR. ROOM

STUDY
13'6"X11'0"

BOOKCASE

MASTER BEDROOM
18'0"X18'0"

DW.

OVENS

PANTRY

BREAKFAST BAR

STOR.

CHINA

BREAKFAST AREA
12'8"X11'0"

DINING ROOM
16'0"X14'0"

SILVER

UP

FOYER

LIBRARY
16'0"X16'0"

BOOKCASE

BOOKS

HER WARDROBE

HIS WARDROBE

W.C.

LINEN

MASTER BATH

SHOWER

WHIRLPOOL TUB

PORCH

The Ashley—Design Q151

The Ashley, a home of elegant Georgian architecture, is reminiscent of the grand homes in the battery section of Charleston, South Carolina. Horse-drawn carriages pass along the streets, seagulls circle overhead and lovers stroll hand-in-hand along the waterfront today, just as they did the day before and the day before that.

Twin Oaks—Design Q152

As the day dawned on their anniversary, her husband suggested a drive in the country. The car turned down a tree-lined drive and there, in front of her, was Twin Oaks—the handsome brick Federal home she had always loved. Now it is theirs, the best gift he could have given her. Evenings are quietly spent sharing the day's events, reading in companionable silence and enjoying the soothing melodies of Beethoven's Moonlight Sonata. This is as good as life gets, and she is in love for the first and last time in her life.

Main Level: 2,187 square feet
Upper Level: 1,118 square feet
Total: 3,305 square feet
Future Recreation Room:
  328 square feet

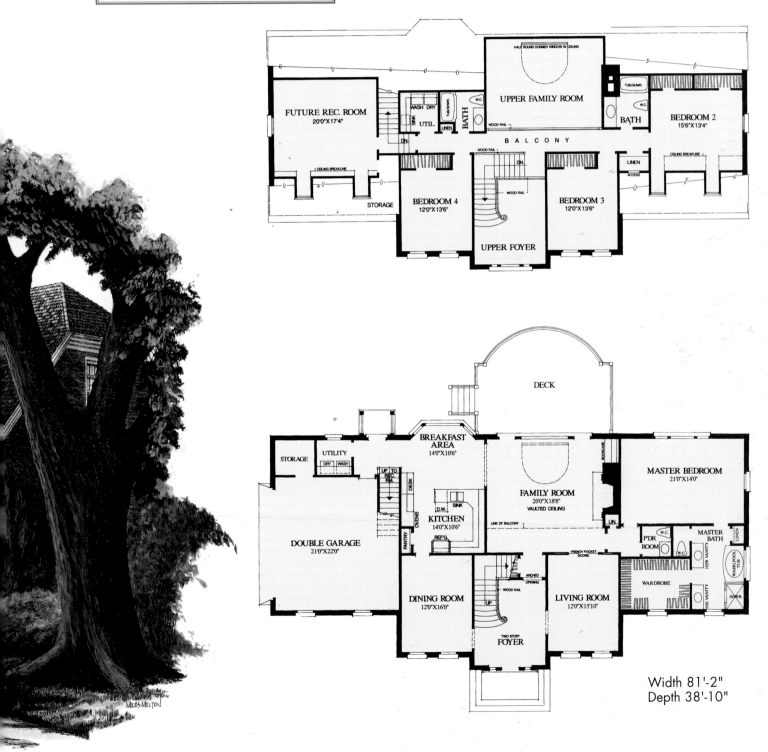

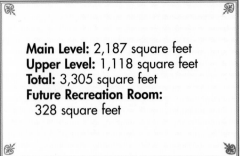

Width 81'-2"
Depth 38'-10"

Main Level: 3,712 square feet
Upper Level: 2,083 square feet
Total: 5,795 square feet
Future Recreation Room:
  409 square feet

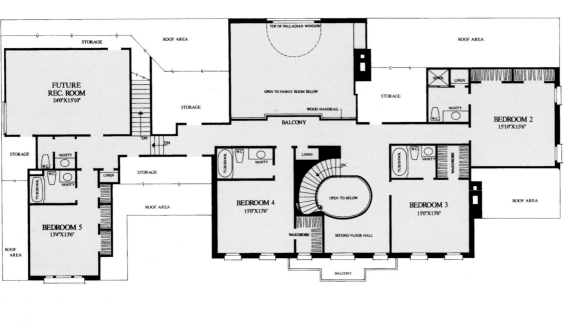

STORAGE

ROOF AREA

TOP OF PALLADIAN WINDOW

ROOF AREA

FUTURE
REC. ROOM
24'0"X15'10"

OPEN TO FAMILY ROOM BELOW

STORAGE

LINEN

SH'R.

STORAGE

WOOD HANDRAIL

STORAGE

VANITY

W.C.

BEDROOM 2
15'10"X15'6"

BALCONY

STORAGE

VANITY

W.C.

LINEN

TUB/SH'R.

W.C.

DN

DN

STORAGE

LINEN

VANITY

W.C.

TUB/SH'R.

DN.

WARDROBE

ROOF AREA

TUB/SH'R.

W.C.

VANITY

ROOF AREA

BEDROOM 4
15'0"X13'6"

OPEN TO BELOW

BEDROOM 3
15'0"X13'6"

BEDROOM 5
13'4"X13'6"

WARDROBE

SECOND FLOOR HALL

ROOF
AREA

BALCONY

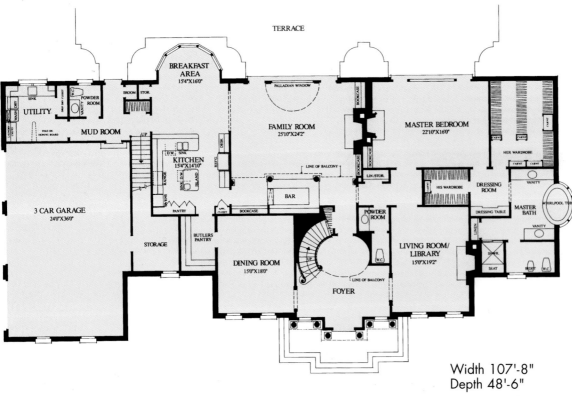

TERRACE

SINK

POWDER
ROOM

VANITY

BREAKFAST
AREA
15'4"X16'0"

BROOM

STOR.

PALLADIAN WINDOW

BOOKCASE

MASTER BEDROOM
22'10"X16'0"

WASH/DRY

UTILITY

FOLD IN
IRONING BOARD

MUD ROOM

UP

FAMILY ROOM
25'10"X24'2"

HER WARDROBE

DESK

D.W.

SINK

KITCHEN
15'4"X14'10"

RANGE

SINK

ISLAND

BAR

REF.

LINE OF BALCONY

BOOKCASE

LIN./STOR.

BOOKCASE

HIS WARDROBE

DRESSING
ROOM

VANITY

MASTER
BATH

WHIRLPOOL TUB

3 CAR GARAGE
24'0"X36'0"

PANTRY

APPL.
CLOSET

BOOKCASE

POWDER
ROOM

DRESSING TABLE

LINEN

VANITY

STORAGE

BUTLERS
PANTRY

UP

W.C.

LIVING ROOM/
LIBRARY
15'0"X19'2"

SH'R.

SEAT

CLOSET

W.C.

DINING ROOM
15'0"X18'0"

FOYER

LINE OF BALCONY

Width 107'-8"
Depth 48'-6"

The Southerly—Design Q153

Climbing bougainvillea, laughing children, swaying Spanish moss, barking dogs, winding paths, trotting horses, tinkling piano keys and mint juleps—a glimpse of The Southerly brings all of these settings and more, to mind. With all of it's grandness and spaciousness, The Southerly is truly a fine example of Southern-style homes.

The Cumberland—Design Q154

Fireworks light the sky with lavish bursts of color. Amid the ooh's and aah's from the crowded gazebo in the town square, we watch the children twirling colorful sparklers in the jet black night—laughing, delighting in the bright circular trails their arms make. Fireworks, sparklers, the 4th of July—what a grand finale to a grand day. We are ever-grateful for our family, our friends and our home— The Cumberland. Life is good.

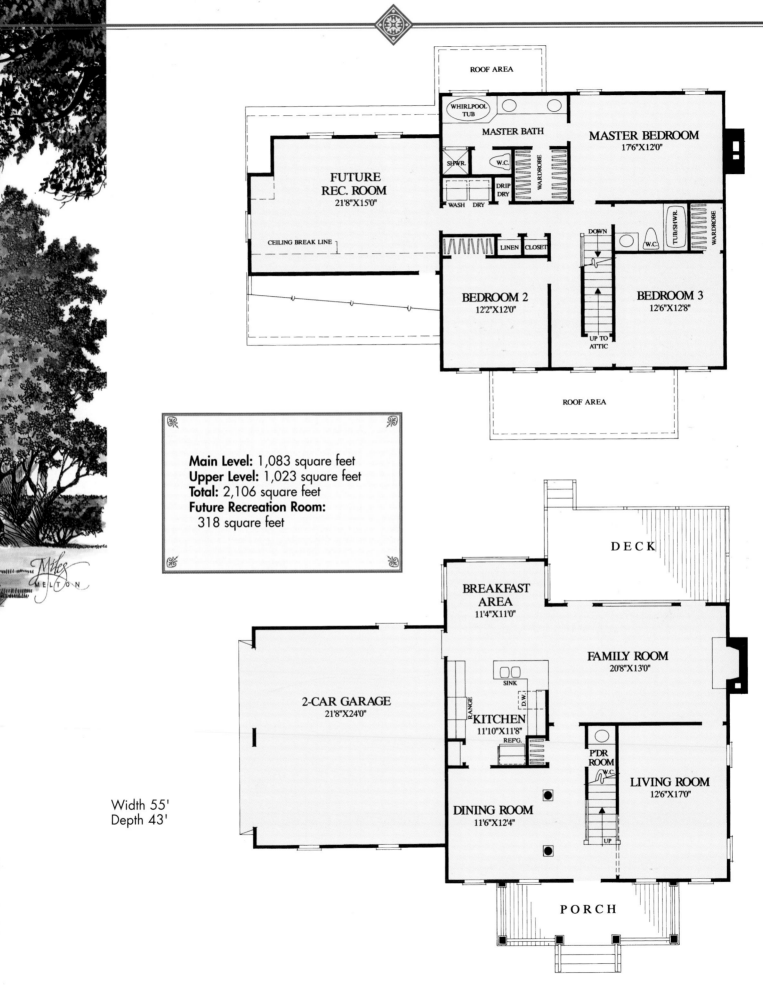

ROOF AREA

WHIRLPOOL TUB

MASTER BATH

MASTER BEDROOM
17'6"X12'0"

SHWR.

W.C.

WARDROBE

FUTURE
REC. ROOM
21'8"X15'0"

DRIP DRY

WASH   DRY

WARDROBE

CEILING BREAK LINE

LINEN   CLOSET

DOWN

TUB/SHWR.

W.C.

BEDROOM 2
12'2"X12'0"

BEDROOM 3
12'6"X12'8"

UP TO ATTIC

ROOF AREA

Main Level: 1,083 square feet
Upper Level: 1,023 square feet
Total: 2,106 square feet
Future Recreation Room:
  318 square feet

DECK

BREAKFAST
AREA
11'4"X11'0"

FAMILY ROOM
20'8"X13'0"

2-CAR GARAGE
21'8"X24'0"

SINK

D.W.

RANGE

KITCHEN
11'10"X11'8"

REF'G.

P'DR
ROOM
W.C.

LIVING ROOM
12'6"X17'0"

DINING ROOM
11'6"X12'4"

UP

Width 55'
Depth 43'

PORCH

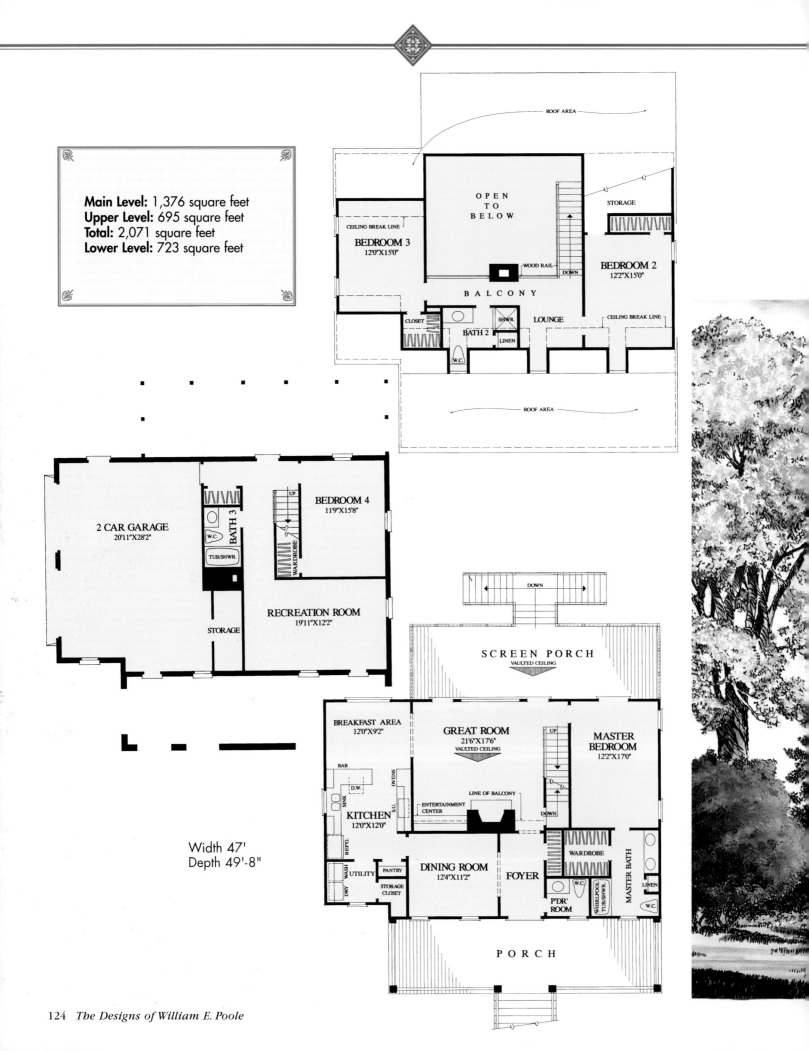

Main Level: 1,376 square feet
Upper Level: 695 square feet
Total: 2,071 square feet
Lower Level: 723 square feet

ROOF AREA

O P E N
T O
B E L O W

STORAGE

CEILING BREAK LINE

BEDROOM 3
12'0"X15'0"

WOOD RAIL

DOWN

BEDROOM 2
12'2"X15'0"

B A L C O N Y

CLOSET

SHWR.

LOUNGE

CEILING BREAK LINE

BATH 2

LINEN

W.C.

ROOF AREA

2 CAR GARAGE
20'11"X28'2"

W.C.

BATH 3

TUB/SHWR.

UP

BEDROOM 4
11'9"X15'8"

WARDROBE

STORAGE

RECREATION ROOM
19'11"X12'2"

DOWN

SCREEN PORCH
VAULTED CEILING

Width 47'
Depth 49'-8"

BREAKFAST AREA
12'0"X9'2"

GREAT ROOM
21'6"X17'6"
VAULTED CEILING

UP

MASTER BEDROOM
12'2"X17'0"

BAR

D.W.

OVENS

ENTERTAINMENT CENTER

LINE OF BALCONY

DOWN

SINK

S.I.I.

KITCHEN
12'0"X12'0"

REF'G.

WARDROBE

WHIRLPOOL TUB/SHWR.

MASTER BATH

LINEN

W.C.

WASH

DRY

UTILITY

PANTRY

STORAGE CLOSET

DINING ROOM
12'4"X11'2"

FOYER

W.C.

P'DR' ROOM

W.C.

P O R C H

Port Royal—Design Q155

*E*very evening after supper, Uncle Henry wanders outdoors to the front porch. He has a ritual from which he never strays. As twilight settles in, he finishes his pipe and slowly unfolds his lanky frame from the creaky rocking chair. He is ready to rosin up his bow and strike the first lively chords of our favorite fiddle tunes. Many pleasant evenings are spent telling tales and making music at The Port Royal.

Currituck Cottage—Design Q156

He was ten years old that first summer at the coast. When the tide was low he could walk all the way to the legendary Rock, examining small sea creatures trapped in the tide-pools. Other times he ran along the high bluffs, or dreamed of pirates and sailing ships. The coastal surroundings of his childhood had a profound effect on his career and he became one of the greatest artists of our time. Artistic demands have extended his travels, but he has never found a place he'd rather be. Currituck Cottage—a home he's comfortable in.

ROOF AREA →

STORAGE

STORAGE

W.C.

DOWN

TUB/SHWR.

BEDROOM 2
15'0"X14'0"

LINEN

BEDROOM 3
13'0"X14'0"

CEILING BREAK LINE

BATH 2

← ROOF AREA

Main Level: 1,554 square feet
Upper Level: 755 square feet
Total: 2,309 square feet
Lower Level: 869 square feet

STORAGE

STORAGE

REC. ROOM
20'7"X16'6"

TUB/SHWR.

W.C.

BATH 4

2 CAR GARAGE
21'0"X24'7"

WARDROBE

BEDROOM 4
12'4"X12'8"

UP

DECK

BREAKFAST AREA
12'0"X10'0"

WHIRLPOOL TUB

SEAT

SHOWER

WARDROBE

GREAT ROOM
20'6"X18'0"

MASTER BATH

BAR

DESK

OVENS

W.C.

LINEN CABINET

P'DR ROOM

W.C.

KITCHEN
11'0"X13'6"

S.U.

SINK

PANTRY

ENTERTAINMENT CENTER

DOWN

MASTER BEDROOM
13'0"X16'8"

D.W.

REF'G.

DRIP DRY

FOLD DN I.B.

DINING ROOM
12'6"X12'6"

DOWN

Width 57'-6"
Depth 39'-6"

SINK

DRY

WASH

FOYER

UP

P O R C H

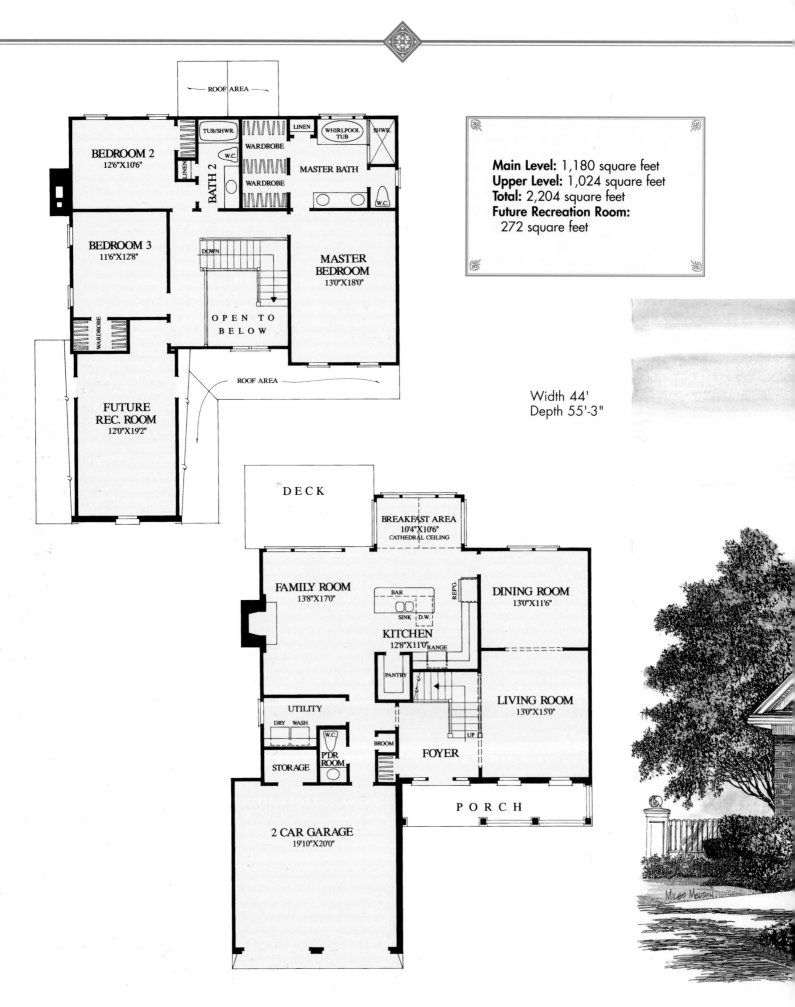

← ROOF AREA →

BEDROOM 2
12'6"X10'6"

TUB/SHWR.

LINEN

WHIRLPOOL TUB

SHWR.

W.C.

WARDROBE

LINEN

BATH 2

MASTER BATH

WARDROBE

WARDROBE

W.C.

BEDROOM 3
11'6"X12'8"

DOWN

OPEN TO BELOW

MASTER BEDROOM
13'0"X18'0"

WARDROBE

ROOF AREA

FUTURE REC. ROOM
12'0"X19'2"

Main Level: 1,180 square feet
Upper Level: 1,024 square feet
Total: 2,204 square feet
Future Recreation Room:
    272 square feet

Width 44'
Depth 55'-3"

DECK

BREAKFAST AREA
10'4"X10'6"
CATHEDRAL CEILING

FAMILY ROOM
13'8"X17'0"

BAR

SINK   D.W.

REFG.

DINING ROOM
13'0"X11'6"

KITCHEN
12'8"X11'0"   RANGE

PANTRY

UTILITY

DRY   WASH

W.C.

BROOM

LIVING ROOM
13'0"X15'0"

UP

STORAGE

P'DR ROOM

FOYER

2 CAR GARAGE
19'10"X20'0"

PORCH

Miles Menton

The Holly Ridge — Design Q157

Suggesting the sentimental charm of the thirties and forties, the Holly Ridge is quaint, charming and affordable. Memories of the milkman delivering ice-cold milk in green glass bottles right to your front door, and the neighbor's child tossing the newspaper from his bicycle make the Holly Ridge reminiscent of homes on any street in any town in America.

Timeless Luxury and Grandeur

*T*here is no question that the homes in Timeless Luxury and Grandeur provide the rich elegance that goes hand-in-hand with the genteel manners of the South. This is not to say that the homes need to be lavish or indulgent. Although if that is your dream, there are an abundance of homes offered throughout the collection that provide the ultimate in opulent style. What makes these homes luxurious is more than just size—their architectural drama, attention to detail and outstanding interior amenities contribute to their world-class style.

All the grandeur of the South shines through in the Richmond Hill (page 136)—a distinguished Plantation-style home. A graceful upper-level balcony invites you to savor the smell of sweetly scented magnolias carried on a soft breeze. This home absolutely revels in elegance and romance.

The dignified, gentle Old-World lifestyle translates well in the Chateau de Bachen (page 140). Whether perched atop the gently rolling hills of the countryside, or at the end of a tree-lined driveway, this home says that you've truly arrived.

While many of the homes in this chapter define the height of comfort and style, others represent luxury of a different sort—an extravagance that is becoming increasingly difficult to come by. In a world that thrives on "busy," it's important to cultivate surroundings that invite relaxation. True luxury is allowing yourself to spend a lazy afternoon, or celebrate the day for no particular reason at all. The homes in this chapter foster all that and more.

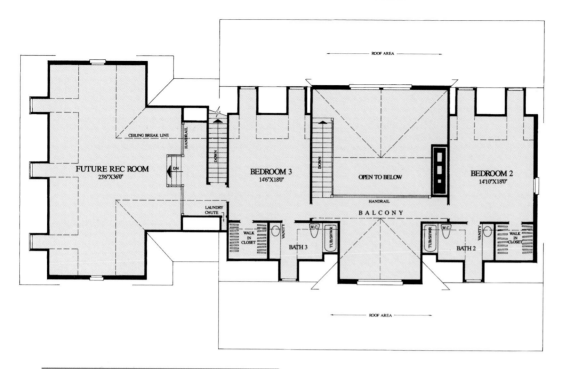

Upper level floor plan labels:

- ROOF AREA
- FUTURE REC ROOM 23'6"X36'0"
- CEILING BREAK LINE
- HANDRAIL
- DN
- DOWN
- BEDROOM 3 14'6"X18'0"
- DOWN
- OPEN TO BELOW
- BEDROOM 2 14'10"X18'0"
- LAUNDRY CHUTE
- BALCONY
- HANDRAIL
- WALK IN CLOSET
- VANITY
- W.C
- TUB/SHWR
- BATH 3
- TUB/SHWR
- W.C
- VANITY
- BATH 2
- WALK IN CLOSET
- ROOF AREA

Main Level: 2,335 square feet
Upper Level: 936 square feet
Total: 3,271 square feet
Future Recreation Room:
  958 square feet
Basement Level: 2,042 square feet

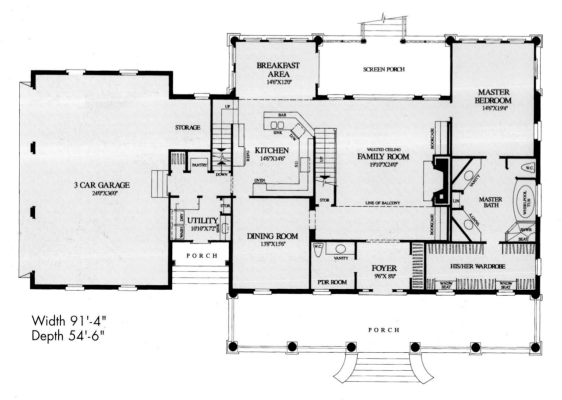

Main level floor plan labels:

- BREAKFAST AREA 14'6"X12'0"
- SCREEN PORCH
- MASTER BEDROOM 14'6"X19'4"
- STORAGE
- UP
- BAR
- SINK
- D/W
- 3 CAR GARAGE 24'0"X36'0"
- PANTRY
- REFG
- KITCHEN 14'6"X14'6"
- STL5
- UP
- VAULTED CEILING FAMILY ROOM 19'10"X24'0"
- BOOKCASE
- W.C
- DOWN
- OVEN
- STOR
- STOR
- LINE OF BALCONY
- VANITY
- LIN
- MASTER BATH
- WHIRLPOOL TUB
- UTILITY 10'10"X7'2"
- WASH DRY SINK
- STOR
- DINING ROOM 13'8"X15'6"
- BOOKCASE
- VANITY
- SHWR SEAT
- PORCH
- W.C
- VANITY
- FOYER 9'6"X8'0"
- HIS/HER WARDROBE
- PDR ROOM
- WNDW SEAT
- WNDW SEAT
- PORCH

Width 91'-4"
Depth 54'-6"

The Airlie—Design Q158

In a tranquil setting down by the waterway is The Airlie. Weddings in the chapel, festivities on the grounds and strolls among the gardens are memories to be treasured by more than just a few. Huge live oaks, masses of azaleas in an amazing array of color and open patches of sun-drenched grassy areas surround this lovely home.

Bromley Court—Design Q159

Never have I seen such gentle and lush countryside as the rolling hills of England. It is today as it must have been throughout the yesterdays—sheep grazing, stone walls and quaint little villages along the way. Now and then a great house appears—classic, balanced, and elegant in detail. Such is the Bromley Court, a very English Georgian dwelling.

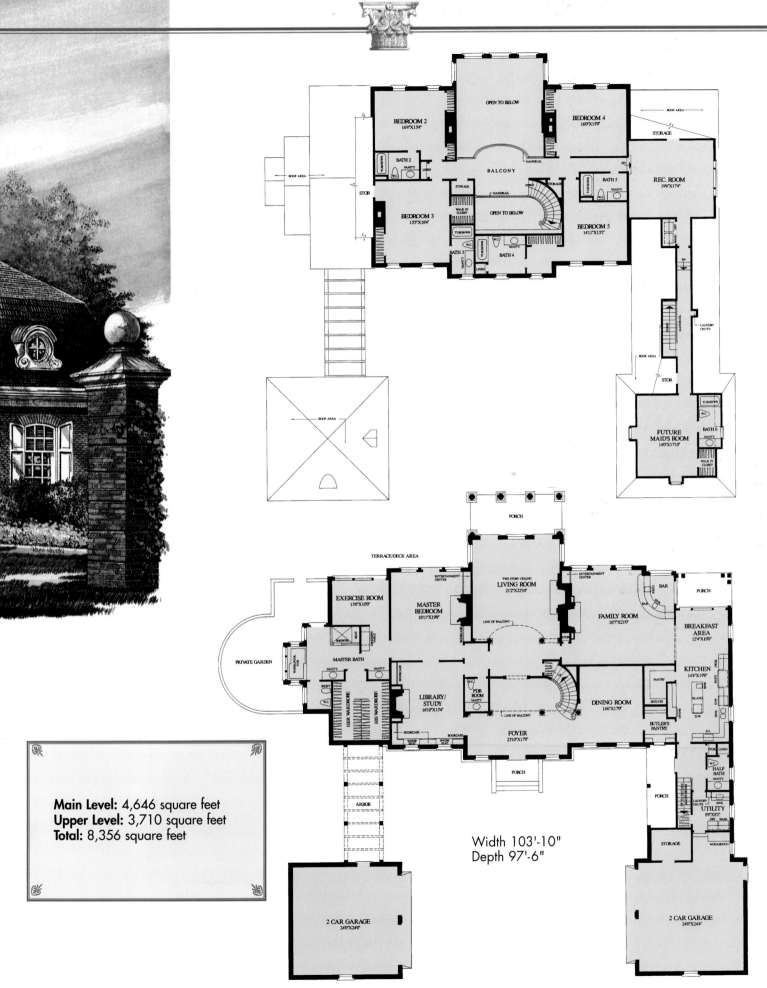

Upper Level Floor Plan:

BEDROOM 2
16'4"X13'4"

OPEN TO BELOW

BEDROOM 4
16'0"X15'0"

ROOF AREA

STORAGE

BATH 2

VANITY

LINEN

RUBSHOWER

W.C.

BALCONY

REC. ROOM
19'6"X17'4"

ROOF AREA

STOR

STORAGE

WALK IN CLOSET

HANDRAIL

STORAGE

BATH 5

RUBSHOWER

VANITY

W.C.

DN

BEDROOM 3
13'5"X18'4"

OPEN TO BELOW

RUBSHOWER

W.C.

VANITY

BEDROOM 5
14'11"X13'2"

BATH 3

VANITY

WALK IN CLOSET

W.C.

VANITY

BATH 4

LINEN

ROOF AREA

DN

HANDRAIL

LAUNDRY CHUTE

ROOF AREA

ROOF AREA

STOR

FUTURE MAID'S ROOM
14'0"X17'10"

BATH 6

RUBSHOWER

W.C.

VANITY

WALK IN CLOSET

Main Level Floor Plan:

PORCH

TERRACE/DECK AREA

EXERCISE ROOM
13'0"X10'0"

ENTERTAINMENT CENTER

LIVING ROOM
21'2"X22'10"
TWO STORY CEILING

ENTERTAINMENT CENTER

BAR

PORCH

MASTER BEDROOM
18'11"X19'8"

FAMILY ROOM
26'7"X21'0"

BREAKFAST AREA
12'4"X10'0"

PRIVATE GARDEN

BOOKCASE

LINE OF BALCONY

KITCHEN
14'4"X19'8"

DESK

WHIRLPOOL TUB

SHOWER
SEAT

DRESSING TABLE

MASTER BATH

VANITY

VANITY

BOOKCASE

W.C.

PDR ROOM
VANITY

STOR

ISLAND

PANTRY

SHELVES

OVENS

SINK

D/W

REFRIG

BIDET

HER WARDROBE

HIS WARDROBE

LIBRARY/STUDY
16'10"X15'4"

DINING ROOM
14'6"X17'0"

BUTLER'S PANTRY

W.C.

BOOKCASE

WINDOW SEAT

BOOKCASE

WINDOW SEAT

LINE OF BALCONY

FOYER
23'10"X17'0"

STOR

LINEN

HALF BATH

VANITY

W.C.

LAUNDRY CHUTE

PORCH

PORCH

UTILITY
8'5"X9'2"

DRY

WASH

ARBOR

STORAGE

STORAGE

WORKBENCH

2 CAR GARAGE
24'0"X24'0"

2 CAR GARAGE
24'0"X24'4"

Width 103'-10"
Depth 97'-6"

Main Level: 4,646 square feet
Upper Level: 3,710 square feet
Total: 8,356 square feet

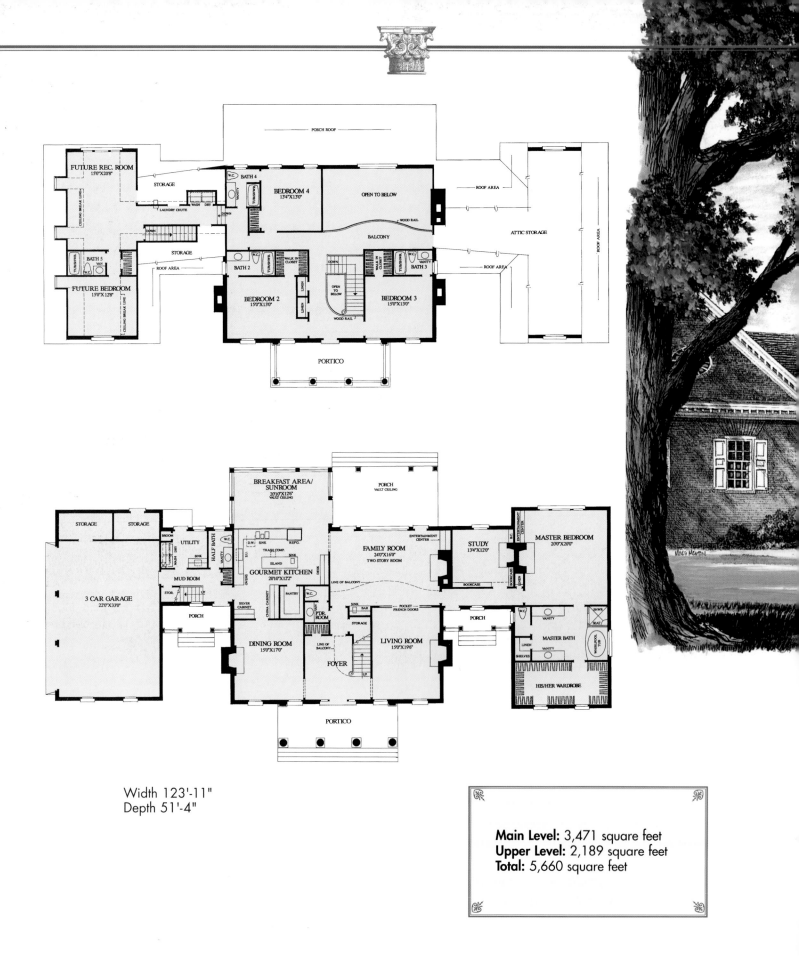

Upper Level

FUTURE REC. ROOM
15'0"X20'8"

STORAGE

BATH 4

BEDROOM 4
13'4"X13'0"

OPEN TO BELOW

ROOF AREA

ROOF AREA

ATTIC STORAGE

LAUNDRY CHUTE

WASH DRY

DOWN

DOWN

WALK IN CLOSET

BALCONY

WOOD RAIL

BATH 5

VAN

STORAGE

BATH 2

OPEN TO BELOW

WALK IN CLOSET

BATH 3

ROOF AREA

FUTURE BEDROOM
15'0"X12'8"

ROOF AREA

BEDROOM 2
15'0"X13'0"

LINEN

LINEN

DOWN

WOOD RAIL

BEDROOM 3
15'0"X13'0"

PORCH ROOF

PORTICO

Main Level

STORAGE

STORAGE

BROOM

UTILITY

HALF BATH

BREAKFAST AREA/ SUNROOM
20'0"X12'6"
VAULT CEILING

PORCH
VAULT CEILING

D.W. SINK REFG.

ISLAND

SINK

MASTER BEDROOM
20'0"X20'0"

ENTERTAINMENT CENTER

FAMILY ROOM
24'0"X16'0"
TWO STORY ROOM

ENTERTAINMENT CENTER

STUDY
13'4"X12'0"

SINK

MUD ROOM

3 CAR GARAGE
22'0"X33'0"

STOR.

UP

GOURMET KITCHEN
20'0"X12'2"

DESK

PANTRY

W.C.

LINE OF BALCONY

BOOKCASE

BOOKCASE

LINEN

PORCH

SILVER CABINET

CHINA CABINET

PDR. ROOM

SINK BAR

STORAGE

POCKET FRENCH DOORS

SINK

W.C.

VANITY

MASTER BATH

VANITY

WHEELDOOR TUB

DINING ROOM
15'0"X17'0"

LINE OF BALCONY

FOYER

UP

LIVING ROOM
15'0"X19'6"

PORCH

LINEN

SHELVES

VANITY

HIS/HER WARDROBE

PORTICO

Width 123'-11"
Depth 51'-4"

Main Level: 3,471 square feet
Upper Level: 2,189 square feet
Total: 5,660 square feet

Richmond Hill—Design Q160

High atop a hill overlooking the James River sits a grand and glorious plantation house. The spectacular views of stars, moon and twinkling lights from the town below entrance visitors from far and near as they gather each evening to recount the adventures of their day and delight in the glories of the night.

The Hamptons—Design Q161

Shingle-style, traditional and modern—as diverse as these descriptions are, they are each appropriate for this uniquely handsome blending of both the old and the new in the Hamptons. The dramatic setting along the shore of Long Island is unrivaled in its beauty, solitude, serenity and paradoxically, its immediate proximity to the city and all that it offers. The Hamptons—the best of all worlds, here for you.

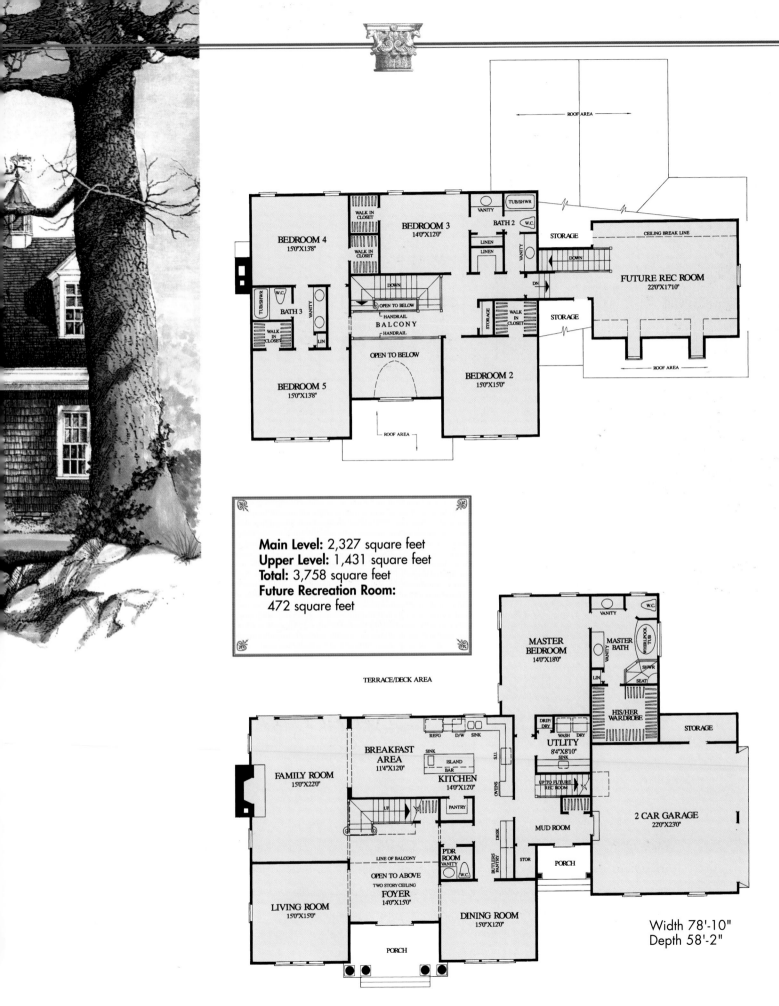

BEDROOM 4
15'0"X13'8"

WALK IN CLOSET

WALK IN CLOSET

BEDROOM 3
14'0"X12'0"

VANITY

TUB/SHWR

BATH 2

W.C.

LINEN

LINEN

VANITY

STORAGE

DOWN

DOWN

DN

CEILING BREAK LINE

FUTURE REC ROOM
22'0"X17'10"

TUB/SHWR

W.C.

BATH 3

VANITY

WALK IN CLOSET

LIN

DOWN

OPEN TO BELOW

HANDRAIL

BALCONY

HANDRAIL

STORAGE

WALK IN CLOSET

STORAGE

ROOF AREA

BEDROOM 5
15'0"X13'8"

OPEN TO BELOW

ROOF AREA

BEDROOM 2
15'0"X15'0"

Main Level: 2,327 square feet
Upper Level: 1,431 square feet
Total: 3,758 square feet
Future Recreation Room:
 472 square feet

TERRACE/DECK AREA

MASTER BEDROOM
14'0"X18'0"

VANITY

W.C.

VANITY

MASTER BATH

WHIRLPOOL TUB

LIN

SHWR

SEAT

HIS/HER WARDROBE

FAMILY ROOM
15'0"X22'0"

BREAKFAST AREA
11'4"X12'0"

REFG

D/W

SINK

SINK

ISLAND

BAR

KITCHEN
14'0"X12'0"

S.U.

OVENS

PANTRY

DRIP/DRY

WASH

DRY

UTILITY
8'4"X8'10"

SINK

STORAGE

UP TO FUTURE REC ROOM

2 CAR GARAGE
22'0"X23'0"

LINE OF BALCONY

LIVING ROOM
15'0"X15'0"

OPEN TO ABOVE

TWO STORY CEILING

FOYER
14'0"X15'0"

PDR ROOM

VANITY

W.C.

BUTLERS PANTRY

DESK

MUD ROOM

STOR

PORCH

DINING ROOM
15'0"X12'0"

PORCH

Width 78'-10"
Depth 58'-2"

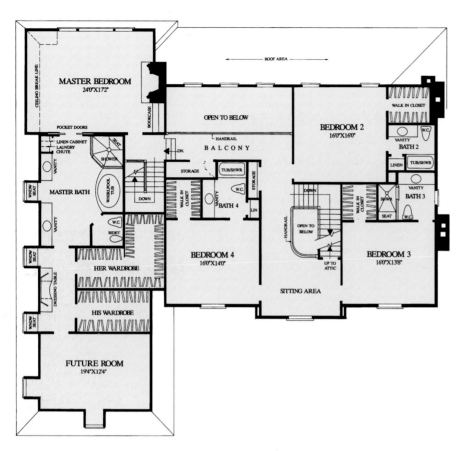

MASTER BEDROOM
24'0"X17'2"

CEILING BREAK LINE

POCKET DOORS

LINEN CABINET
LAUNDRY
CHUTE

VANITY

MASTER BATH

WINDOW
SEAT

VANITY

WINDOW
SEAT

DRESSING TABLE

WINDOW
SEAT

HER WARDROBE

HIS WARDROBE

FUTURE ROOM
19'4"X12'4"

BOOKCASE

SEAT

SHOWER

WHIRLPOOL
TUB

DOWN

W.C

BIDET

OPEN TO BELOW

HANDRAIL

BALCONY

DN.

STORAGE

TUB/SHWR

W.C.

VANITY

BATH 4

LIN

WALK IN CLOSET

ROOF AREA

BEDROOM 2
16'0"X16'0"

WALK IN CLOSET

VANITY

W.C

BATH 2

LINEN

TUB/SHWR

VANITY

BATH 3

SHWR

SEAT

W.C.

DOWN

HANDRAIL

OPEN TO BELOW

UP TO ATTIC

WALK IN CLOSET

STORAGE

STORAGE

BEDROOM 4
16'0"X14'0"

BEDROOM 3
16'0"X13'8"

SITTING AREA

Main Level: 2,870 square feet
Upper Level: 2,502 square feet
Total: 5,372 square feet

TERRACEE/DECK AREA

BATH 5

VAN

W.C.

TUB/SHWR

BEDROOM 5
16'8"X17'0"

WALK IN CLOSET

DRIP/
DRY

WASH DRY

LAUNDRY
CHUTE

SINK

UTILITY
12'4"X8'0"

LINEN

STORAGE

KITCHEN
15'0"X18'2"
VOLUME CEILING

D/W SINK

SLU

D/W

ISLAND

OVENS

REFG

BREAKFAST
AREA
9'0"X18'2"
VOLUME CEILING

LINE OF BALCONY

DESK

PANTRY

W.C.

BUTLERS
PANTRY

VANITY

P'DR ROOM

UP

STORAGE

LINE OF BALCONY

DINING ROOM
16'0"X18'0"

BAR

SHELVES

UP

FOYER
14'0"X18'0"

BOOKCASE

FAMILY ROOM
24'8"X20'2"

BOOKCASE

LIVING ROOM
16'0"X24'0"

3 CAR GARAGE
24'0"X34'10"

STOOP

Width 72'
Depth 66'-6"

Chateau De Bachen—Design Q162

Evenly spaced trees lining the way, fields of lavender light and the smell of freshly cut hay—these sights and smells engulfed our senses as we approached Chateau De Bachen. The impressive simplicity, the massive presence, the natural melding of architecture and landscape seemed so right, so romantic, so perfect. An intimate getaway for our very first night together.

Upper Level

FUTURE REC ROOM
19'4"X18'0"

STORAGE

STORAGE

ROOF AREA

BEDROOM 3
15'0"X11'4"

VANITY
BATH 3
VANITY
W.C.
LIN
TUB/SHWR

BEDROOM 4
13'8"X11'4"

LIN

WALK IN CLOSET

WOOD BEAMS

OPEN TO BELOW

WOOD BEAMS

BALCONY

HANDRAIL

OPEN TO BELOW

DOWN

ROOF AREA

STOR

BEDROOM 2
14'8"X12'0"

VANITY
WALK IN CLOSET

TUB/SHWR
BATH 2
LIN
W.C.

ROOF AREA

Main Level

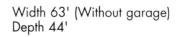
WOOD TRELLIS

TERRACE

2 CAR GARAGE
24'0"X24'0"

STORAGE

PORCH

UTILITY
8'0"X5'0"
SINK
DRY WASH
DRIP DRY
REF/REACH

PANTRY

KITCHEN
15'8"X11'0"

OPENS

BAR
ISLAND

REFRG

DW

SUB

WOOD BEAMS

BREAKFAST AREA
13'6"X10'0"

PDR ROOM
VANITY
W.C.

DINING ROOM
15'0"X14'0"

BOOKCASE

ARCHED OPENING

BOOKCASE

FOYER
13'6"X13'6"

STOOP

UP

OPEN TO ABOVE

CATHEDRAL CEILING
GREAT ROOM
18'6"X26'0"

BOOKCASE

MASTER BEDROOM
18'0"X17'10"

W.C.

WHIRLPOOL TUB
MASTER BATH

VANITY
LIN

HIS/HER WARDROBE

VANITY

SHWR
SEAT

Width 63' (Without garage)
Depth 44'

Main Level: 2,207 square feet
Upper Level: 1,098 square feet
Total: 3,305 square feet
Playroom: 402 square feet

Le Mans—Design Q163

The door opened and we were greeted by a most gracious and lovely lady, the owner of Le Mans. Indeed, her family had lived here for generations and it was only recently that she began using the first floor to display her antiques. Exquisite and elegant pieces—each a treasure, much like the home itself. A memory not to be forgotten, but displayed and enjoyed now and always.

Les Serein—Design Q164

With hair flying and cheeks rosy, the lady of Les Serein pedaled her bicycle through the winding streets of town. Along her travels, greetings were exchanged with passing neighbors as they made their way—as they did every morning—to and from the bakery. In some places, some things never change, nor should they.

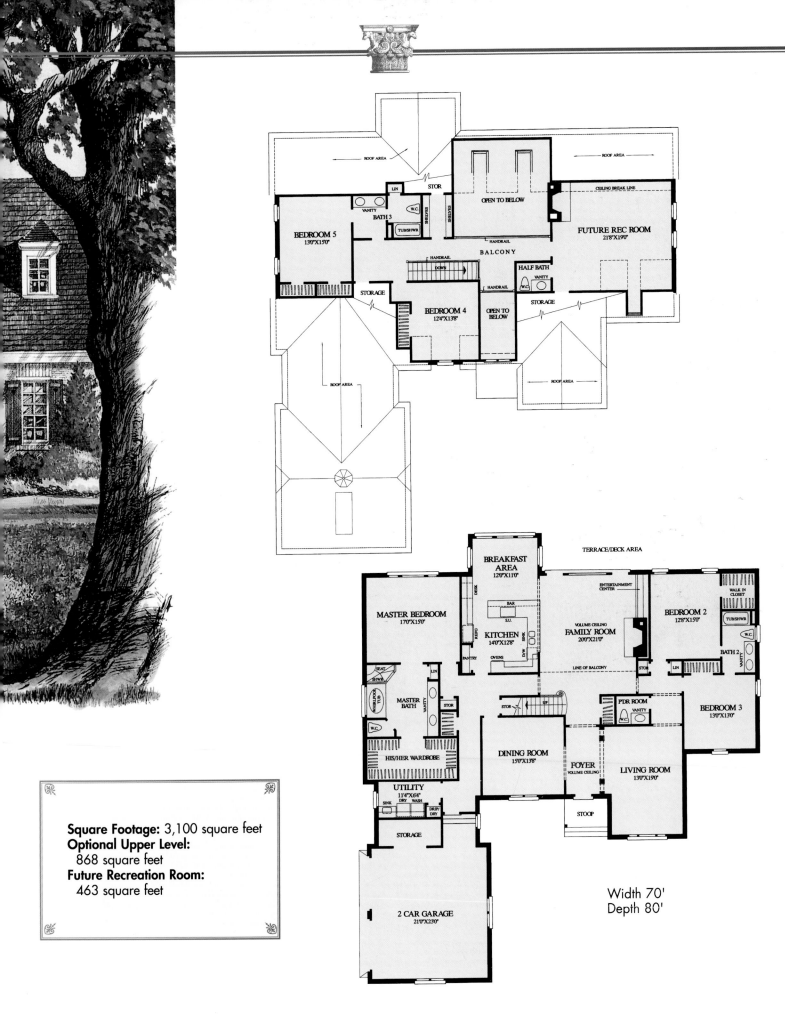

ROOF AREA   ROOF AREA

LIN   STOR

VANITY

BATH 3

W.C.

SHELVES

TUB/SHWR

OPEN TO BELOW

CEILING BREAK LINE

BEDROOM 5
13'0"X15'0"

FUTURE REC ROOM
21'8"X19'0"

BALCONY

HANDRAIL

HANDRAIL   DOWN

HALF BATH

W.C.   VANITY

STORAGE

STORAGE

BEDROOM 4
12'4"X13'8"

OPEN TO BELOW

STORAGE

ROOF AREA

ROOF AREA

ROOF AREA

BREAKFAST AREA
12'0"X11'0"

TERRACE/DECK AREA

ENTERTAINMENT CENTER

WALK IN CLOSET

MASTER BEDROOM
17'0"X15'0"

BAR
S.U.

REF.

SINK

KITCHEN
14'0"X12'8"

VOLUME CEILING
FAMILY ROOM
20'0"X21'0"

BEDROOM 2
12'8"X15'0"

TUB/SHWR

W.C.

PANTRY

OVENS

D/W

LINE OF BALCONY

STOR

BATH 2

LIN

VANITY

SEAT

SHWR

LIN

STOR

STOR

UP

PDR ROOM

W.C.

VANITY

BEDROOM 3
13'0"X13'0"

WHIRLPOOL TUB

MASTER BATH

VANITY

W.C.

HIS/HER WARDROBE

DINING ROOM
15'0"X13'8"

FOYER
VOLUME CEILING

LIVING ROOM
13'0"X19'0"

UTILITY
11'4"X6'4"
DRY   WASH

SINK

DRIP/DRY

STORAGE

STOOP

2 CAR GARAGE
21'0"X23'0"

Square Footage: 3,100 square feet
Optional Upper Level:
  868 square feet
Future Recreation Room:
  463 square feet

Width 70'
Depth 80'

Bay St. Louis—Design Q165

The Bay St. Louis sits upon a grassy knoll overlooking the bay. The setting is serene, the massive trees are old and the lapping waters on the white sandy beaches are soothing. However, the serenity is subject to drastic change as our children, young parents with their children in tow, arrive to spend another delightful summer at home in the Bay St. Louis.

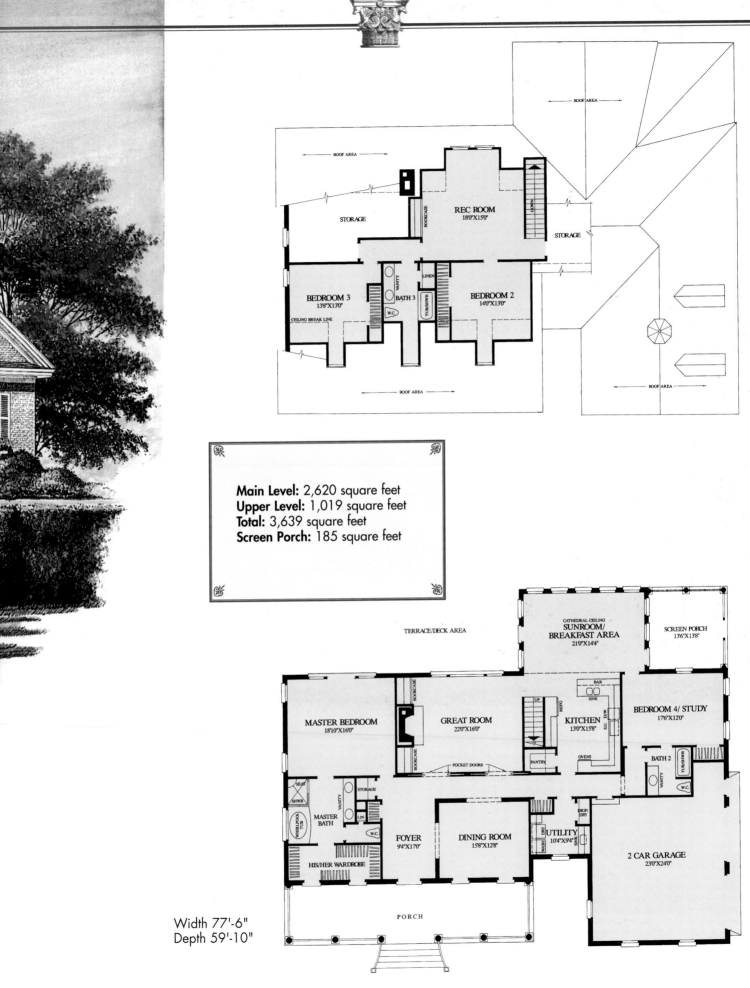

STORAGE

REC ROOM
18'0"X15'0"

STORAGE

BOOKCASE

DOWN

ROOF AREA

ROOF AREA

ROOF AREA

ROOF AREA

ROOF AREA

BEDROOM 3
13'8"X13'0"

VANITY

BATH 3

W.C.

TUB/SHWR

LINEN

BEDROOM 2
14'0"X13'0"

CEILING BREAK LINE

Main Level: 2,620 square feet
Upper Level: 1,019 square feet
Total: 3,639 square feet
Screen Porch: 185 square feet

TERRACE/DECK AREA

CATHEDRAL CEILING
**SUNROOM/
BREAKFAST AREA**
21'0"X14'4"

SCREEN PORCH
13'6"X13'8"

MASTER BEDROOM
18'10"X16'0"

GREAT ROOM
22'0"X16'0"

BOOKCASE

BOOKCASE

UP.

BAR

SINK

FRIG.

KITCHEN
13'0"X15'8"

STL.

D/W

BEDROOM 4/ STUDY
17'6"X12'0"

POCKET DOORS

PANTRY

OVENS

BATH 2

VANITY

W.C.

SEAT

SHWR

WHIRLPOOL TUB

MASTER BATH

VANITY

LIN

W.C.

STORAGE

FOYER
9'4"X17'0"

DINING ROOM
15'8"X12'8"

WASH

DRY

UTILITY
10'4"X9'4"

DRIP/
DRY

SINK

2 CAR GARAGE
23'0"X24'0"

HIS/HER WARDROBE

PORCH

Width 77'-6"
Depth 59'-10"

Abbeville—Design Q166

She was an independent woman, a witty and caring woman who had lived in the Abbeville for so long that she was thought of as "one" with her home. Stories abound, like the day she was in a hurry but needed to stop at the bank. Due to unavailable parking space, she left her car in the middle of the road. A new policeman—not knowing the "do's" and "dont's" of a small town—was stopped in the nick of time from writing her a ticket. As the bank president stepped out front, he smiled, waved away the ticket and explained, "Miss Lottie lives in the Abbeville."

Main Level: 2,993 square feet
Upper Level: 1,452 square feet
Total: 4,445 square feet
Future Recreation Room:
  611 square feet
Screen Porch: 266 square feet

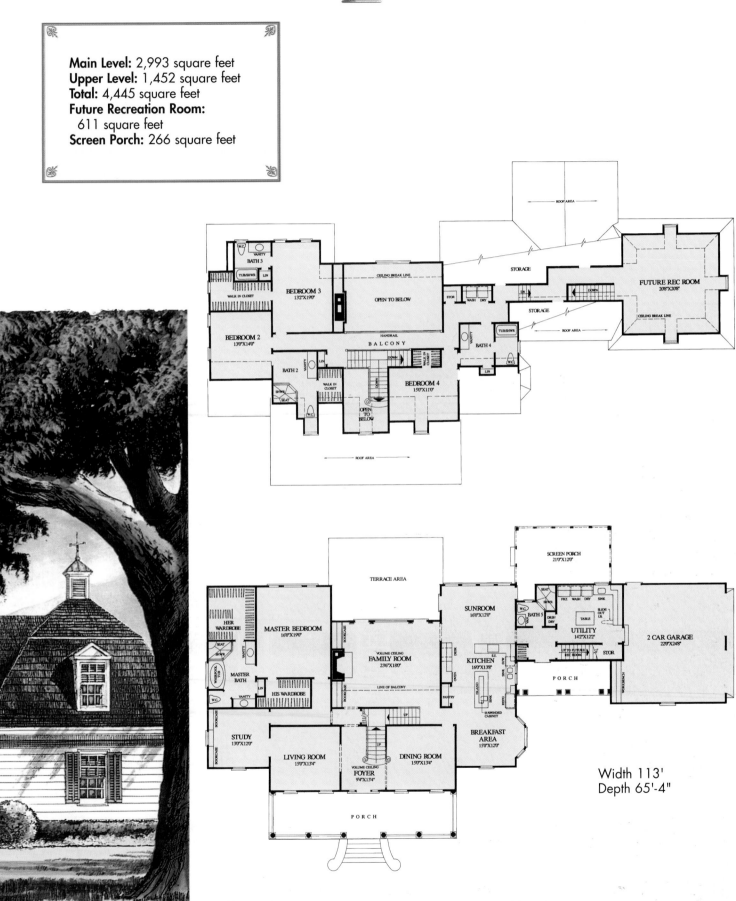

Width 113'
Depth 65'-4"

Main Level: 2,986 square feet
Upper Level: 1,260 square feet
Total: 4,246 square feet
Future Recreation Room &
Bedroom 5: 758 square feet

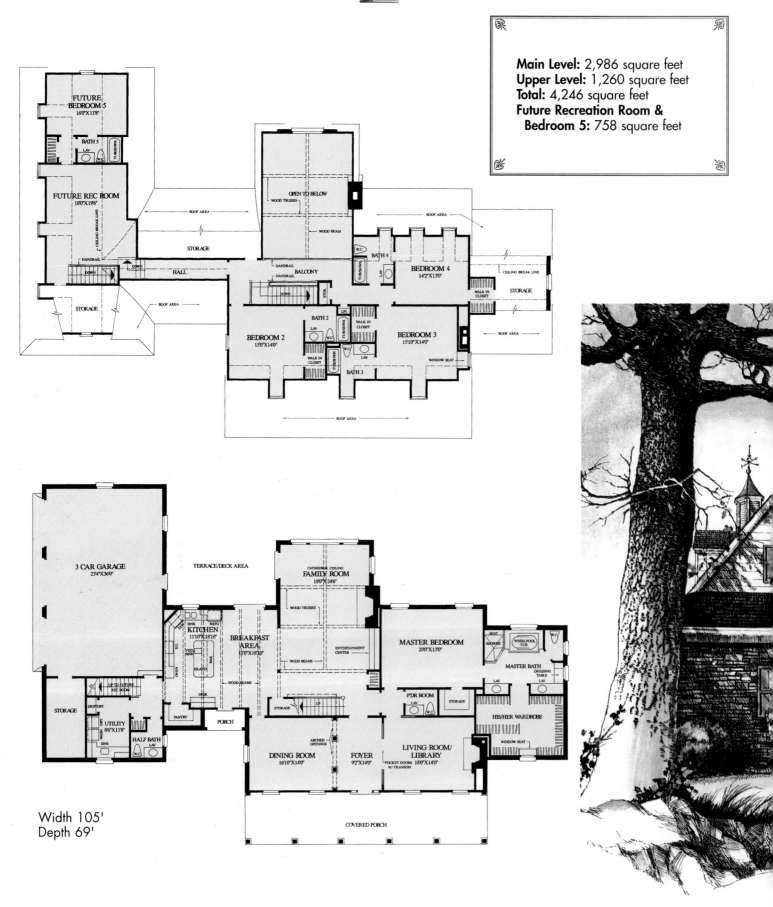

FUTURE BEDROOM 5
16'0"X11'8"

BATH 5
LAV
W.C.
TUB/SHWR

FUTURE REC ROOM
18'0"X19'6"

CEILING BREAK LINE

ROOF AREA

STORAGE

OPEN TO BELOW
WOOD TRUSSES

WOOD BEAM

ROOF AREA

W.C.
BATH 4
TUB/SHWR
LAV

BEDROOM 4
14'2"X13'0"

CEILING BREAK LINE

STORAGE

HANDRAIL
DOWN
DOWN
HALL

HANDRAIL
BALCONY
HANDRAIL
DOWN

WALK IN CLOSET

ROOF AREA

WALK IN CLOSET

STORAGE

ROOF AREA

STORAGE

BATH 2
LAV
W.C.
LIN.
TUB/SHWR

WALK IN CLOSET
LAV

BEDROOM 2
15'0"X14'0"

W.C.

BEDROOM 3
15'10"X14'0"

WALK IN CLOSET
TUB/SHWR
LAV
HANDRAIL
BATH 3

WINDOW SEAT

ROOF AREA

3 CAR GARAGE
23'4"X36'0"

TERRACE/DECK AREA

CATHEDRAL CEILING
FAMILY ROOM
18'0"X24'6"

WOOD TRUSSES

SINK
REF.
KITCHEN
11'10"X18'0"

BREAKFAST AREA
11'0"X18'0"

ENTERTAINMENT CENTER

MASTER BEDROOM
20'0"X15'0"

SEAT
SHOWER
WHIRLPOOL TUB
LAV

VEG SINK
OVEN
ISLAND
BAR

WOOD BEAMS

WOOD BEAMS

MASTER BATH
DRESSING TABLE
LAV

STORAGE

UP TO FUTURE REC ROOM

DESK

UTILITY
8'6"X11'8"
SINK

PANTRY

PORCH

STORAGE

P'DR ROOM
LAV
W.C.

STORAGE

HIS/HER WARDROBE

HALF BATH
LAV
W.C.

ARCHED OPENINGS

DINING ROOM
16'10"X14'0"

FOYER
9'2"X14'0"

LIVING ROOM/ LIBRARY
18'0"X14'0"
POCKET DOORS W/ TRANSOM

WINDOW SEAT

COVERED PORCH

Width 105'
Depth 69'

Hudson Valley—Design Q167

*O*ut on the trail, exhilarated by the pounding hooves beneath me and crisp morning air, I turn my mount towards home, a warm crackling fire and breakfast. As we draw near, smoke spirals from the chimney and my mouth waters in anticipation of sausages and eggs. The warmth, charm and texture of my beloved retreat greets me, as always. The best place I could ever hope to be — The Hudson Valley, my Dutch Colonial home.

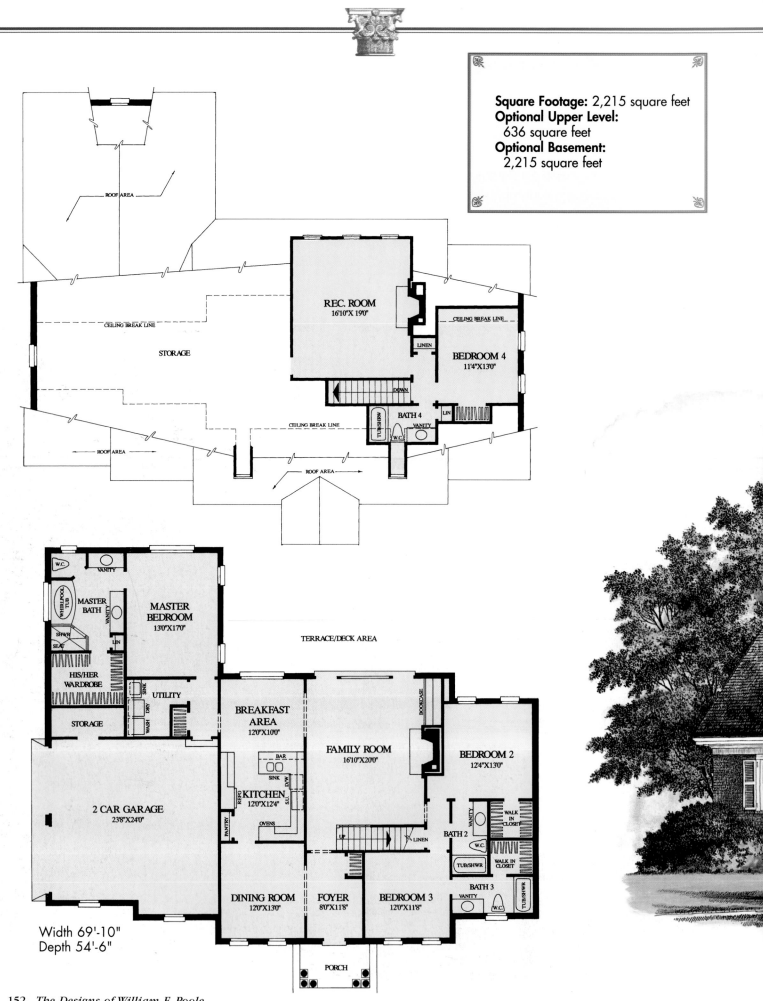

Square Footage: 2,215 square feet
Optional Upper Level:
636 square feet
Optional Basement:
2,215 square feet

ROOF AREA

REC. ROOM
16'10"X 19'0"

CEILING BREAK LINE

STORAGE

LINEN

CEILING BREAK LINE

BEDROOM 4
11'4"X13'0"

DOWN

ROOF AREA

CEILING BREAK LINE

TUB/SHWR

BATH 4

LIN

W.C.

VANITY

ROOF AREA

W.C.

VANITY

WHIRLPOOL TUB

MASTER BATH

VANITY

MASTER BEDROOM
13'0"X17'0"

TERRACE/DECK AREA

SHWR

SEAT

LIN

HIS/HER WARDROBE

STORAGE

SINK

DRY

WASH

UTILITY

BREAKFAST AREA
12'0"X10'0"

FAMILY ROOM
16'10"X20'0"

BOOKCASE

BEDROOM 2
12'4"X13'0"

BAR

SINK

D.W.

2 CAR GARAGE
23'8"X24'0"

REFG

PANTRY

KITCHEN
12'0"X12'4"

S.U.

OVENS

UP

DOWN

LINEN

VANITY

WALK IN CLOSET

W.C.

BATH 2

TUB/SHWR

WALK IN CLOSET

DINING ROOM
12'0"X13'0"

FOYER
8'0"X11'8"

BEDROOM 3
12'0"X11'8"

BATH 3

VANITY

W.C.

TUB/SHWR

Width 69'-10"
Depth 54'-6"

PORCH

Valdosta—Design Q168

Miss Margaret has lived here all her life—along with her brothers, sisters, cousins and grandparents. The Valdosta has been their home forever. It is with many fond memories that she bids a final farewell to the Valdosta with an abundance of good wishes, happiness and joy for the new family ready to create a fresh family history within their new home. Here's to grand memories and new beginnings.

St. Francisville—Design Q169

If you have never been to St. Francisville, you must go—especially during their annual spring Audubon pilgrimage. This quaint little town is resplendent in color with flowers, flags, costumes from another era and strolling visitors such you and me. A welcoming village filled with historic homes such as this, all still there for us to see.

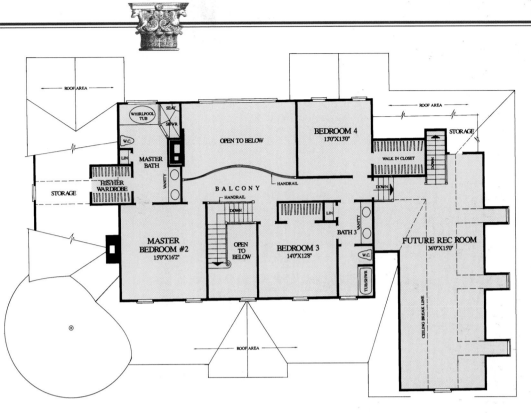

Upper level floor plan labels:
- ROOF AREA
- WHIRLPOOL TUB
- SEAT
- SHWR
- W.C.
- OPEN TO BELOW
- BEDROOM 4 13'0"X13'0"
- ROOF AREA
- STORAGE
- LIN
- MASTER BATH
- VANITY
- WALK IN CLOSET
- STORAGE
- HIS/HER WARDROBE
- BALCONY
- HANDRAIL
- DOWN
- MASTER BEDROOM #2 15'0"X16'2"
- HANDRAIL
- DOWN
- OPEN TO BELOW
- BEDROOM 3 14'0"X12'8"
- LIN
- BATH 3
- VANITY
- W.C.
- TUB/SHWR
- FUTURE REC ROOM 36'0"X15'0"
- CEILING BREAK LINE
- ROOF AREA

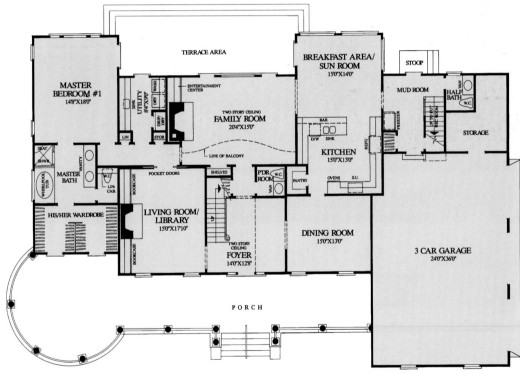

Main level floor plan labels:
- TERRACE AREA
- BREAKFAST AREA/ SUN ROOM 15'0"X14'0"
- STOOP
- MASTER BEDROOM #1 14'8"X18'0"
- SINK
- UTILITY 8'4"X9'0"
- WASH
- DRY
- DRY/DRY
- ENTERTAINMENT CENTER
- MUD ROOM
- HALF BATH
- VAN
- W.C.
- LIN
- STOR
- TWO STORY CEILING
- FAMILY ROOM 20'4"X15'0"
- BAR
- PREEZER
- SEAT
- SHWR
- WHIRLPOOL TUB
- MASTER BATH
- VANITY
- W.C.
- LIN CAB.
- BOOKCASE
- POCKET DOORS
- LINE OF BALCONY
- D/W
- SINK
- KITCHEN 15'0"X13'0"
- REFG
- STORAGE
- HIS/HER WARDROBE
- LIVING ROOM/ LIBRARY 15'0"X17'10"
- BOOKCASE
- SHELVES
- PDR ROOM
- W.C.
- VAN
- PANTRY
- OVENS
- S.U.
- UP TO REC ROOM
- UP
- TWO STORY CEILING
- FOYER 14'0"X12'8"
- DINING ROOM 15'0"X13'0"
- 3 CAR GARAGE 24'0"X36'0"
- PORCH

Width 89'-4"
Depth 60'

Main Level: 2,442 square feet
Upper Level: 1,286 square feet
Total: 3,728 square feet
Future Recreation Room:
  681 square feet

The Blueprint Package

Each set of home plan blueprints is a related gathering of plans, diagrams, measurements, details and specifications that precisely show how your new residence will come together. Each home design receives careful attention and planning from the expert staff of William E. Poole Designs, Inc. to ensure quality and buildability.

Here's what the package includes:

- ◆ Designer's rendering of front elevation
- ◆ Foundation and dimensioned floor plans
- ◆ Building cross sections
- ◆ Selected interior elevations
- ◆ Fireplace, stair, moulding and cabinet details
- ◆ Working drawings of ¼" scale or larger
- ◆ Electrical plans
- ◆ All exterior elevations
- ◆ Door and window sizes
- ◆ Roof plan and exterior details

Reversed plans are mirror-image sets with lettering and dimensioning shown backwards. To receive plans in reverse, specifically request this when placing your order. Since lettering and dimensions appear backward on reverse blueprints, we suggest you order one set reversed for siting and the rest as shown for construction purposes. (See page 158 for additional information.)

Plans are designed to meet the requirements of the *Council of American Building Officials (CABO) One and Two Family Dwelling Code*. Because codes are subject to various changes and interpretations, the purchaser is responsible for compliance with all local building codes, ordinances, site conditions, subdivision restrictions and structural elements by having their builder review the plans to ensure compliance. We also recommend that you have an engineer in your area review your plans before actual construction begins.

☎ ORDER TOLL FREE 1-800-521-6797
After you've looked over The Blueprint Package and Additional Products on the following page, simply mail the order form on page 159 or call toll free on our Blueprint Hotline: **1-800-521-6797**. We're ready and eager to serve you.

Additional Products

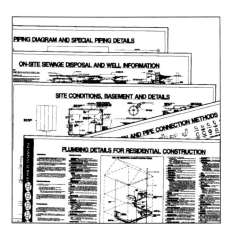

PLUMBING

If you want to know more about the complete plumbing system, these 24x36-inch detail sheets will prove very useful. Prepared to meet requirements of the National Plumbing Code, these six fact-filled sheets give general information on pipe schedules, fittings, sump-pump details, water-softener hookups, septic system details and much more. Color-coded sheets include a glossary of terms.

ELECTRICAL

Prepared to meet requirements of the National Electrical Code, these comprehensive 24x36-inch drawings come packed with helpful information, including wire sizing, switch-installation schematics, cable-routing details, appliance wattage, doorbell hookups, typical service panel circuitry and much more. Six sheets are bound together and color-coded for easy reference. A glossary of terms is also included.

24"x36" BLACK & WHITE RENDERING

Black and white renderings are available for all of the plans contained in this book. For additional information please call the toll-free number listed below.

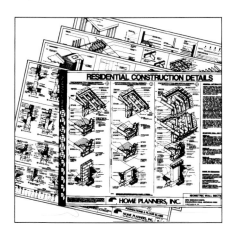

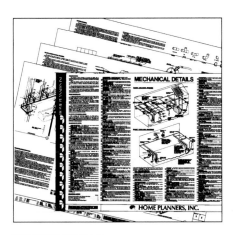

CONSTRUCTION

To help you understand how your house will be built—and offer additional techniques—this set of drawings depicts the materials and methods used to build foundations, fireplaces, walls, floors and roofs. Where appropriate, the drawings show acceptable alternatives. These six sheets will answer questions for the advanced do-it-yourselfer or home planner.

MECHANICAL

This package will help you make informed decisions and communicate with subcontractors about heating and cooling systems. The 24x36-inch drawings contain instructions and samples that allow you to make simple load calculations and preliminary sizing and costing analysis. Covered are today's most commonly used systems from heat pumps to solar fuel systems. The package is full of illustrations and diagrams to help you visualize components and how they relate to one another.

SPECIFICATION OUTLINE

This 16-page document is critical to building your house correctly. Designed to be filled in by you or your builder, this book lists 166 stages or items crucial to the building process. It provides a comprehensive review of the construction process and helps in choosing materials. When combined with the blueprints, a signed contract, and a schedule, it becomes a legal document and record for the building of your home.

To Order, Call Toll Free
1-800-521-6797

To add these important extras to your Blueprint Package, simply indicate your choices on the order form on page 159 or call us toll free 1-800-521-6897.

Price Schedule And Plans Index

Prices Guaranteed Through December 31, 2000

Price Description:

1 Set of Plans	$695
5 Sets of Plans	$795
8 Sets of Plans	$875
Each Additional Set of the Same Plan (within 60 days)	$60
Surcharge for Reverse Sets	$25
Reproducible Vellum	$1,095
24"x36" Black & White Rendering	$50

Note: There is a surcharge of $25 per plan order to reverse any number of sets. Examples: one regular set plus one additional set and one reverse set ($695 + $60 + $25 = $780). Five regular sets and one reverse set ($795 + $25 = $820). Eight regular sets and one reverse set ($875 + $25 = $900) plus shipping and tax, if applicable.

Reproducible Vellums

Reproducible vellums are granted with a non-exclusive license to do the following:

● To modify the drawings for use in the construction of a single home
● To make up to twelve (12) copies of the plans for use in the construction of a single home
● To construct one and only one home based on the plans, either in the original form or as modified by you.

Limitations on use of the plans. You may NOT do any of the following with the reproducible vellum:

● Use the plans in either their original form or as modified to construct more than one home
● Permit others to use or copy the plans
● Make more than twelve (12) copies of the plans (if additional plans are needed you must first obtain written permission)
● Sell, lend or otherwise transfer the plans to another

Index

To use the Index below, refer to the design number listed in numerical order (a helpful page reference is also given). Refer to the price description above for the cost of one, five or eight sets of blueprints or the cost of a reproducible vellum. Additional prices are shown for identical and reverse blueprint sets.

To Order: Fill in and send the order form on page 159—or call toll free 1-800-521-6797 or 520-297-8200.

Title. You have purchased a license to use the plans. The title to and intellectual property rights in the plans shall remain with William E. Poole Designs, Inc. Use of the plans in a manner inconsistent with this agreement is a violation of U.S Copyright laws. These designs are protected under the terms of the United States Copyright Law and may not be copied or reproduced in any way, by any means, unless you have purchased Reproducibles, which clearly indicate your right to copy or reproduce. We authorize the use of your chosen design as an aid in the construction of one single family home only. You may not use this design to build a second or multiple dwellings without purchasing another blueprint or blueprints or paying additional design fees.

Modifications and warranties. Any modifications made to the vellums by parties other than William E. Poole Designs, Inc., voids any warranties express or implied including the warranties of fitness for a particular purpose and merchantability.

Disclaimer
Substantial care and effort have gone into the creation of these blueprints. However, because we cannot provide on-site consultation, supervision and control over actual construction, and because of the great variance in local building requirements, building practices and soil, seismic, weather and other conditions, WE CANNOT MAKE ANY WARRANTY, EXPRESS OR IMPLIED, WITH RESPECT TO THE CONTENT OR USE OF OUR BLUEPRINTS, INCLUDING BUT NOT LIMITED TO ANY WARRANTY OF MERCHANTABILITY OR OF FITNESS FOR A PARTICULAR PURPOSE.

Purchase Policy
Accurate construction-cost estimates should come from your builder after review of the blueprints.
Your purchase includes a license to use the plans to construct one single-family residence.
These plans may NOT be reproduced, modified or used to create derivative works.
Additional sets of the same plan may be ordered within a 60-day period at $60 each, plus shipping and tax, if applicable. After 60 days, re-orders are treated as new orders.

How Many Blueprints Do You Need?
A single set of blueprints is sufficient to study a home in greater detail. However, if you are planning to obtain cost estimates from a contractor or subcontractors—or if you are planning to build immediately—you will need more sets. Because additional sets are less expensive when ordered in quantity with the original order, make sure you order enough blueprints to satisfy all requirements. The following checklist will help you determine how many you need:

___ Owner
___ Builder (generally requires at least three sets; one as a legal document, one to use during inspections, and at least one to give to subcontractors.
___ Local Building Department (often requires two sets)
___ Mortgage Lender (usually one set for a conventional loan; three sets for FHA or VA loans)

___ TOTAL NUMBER OF SETS

Toll Free 1-800-521-6797
Regular Office Hours:
8:00 a.m. to 8:00 p.m. Eastern Time, Monday through Friday
Our staff will gladly answer any questions during regular office hours. Our answering service can place orders after hours or on weekends.
If we receive your order by 4:00 p.m. Eastern Time, Monday through Friday, we'll process it and ship within two business days. When ordering by phone, please have your charge card ready. We'll also ask you for the Order Form Key Number at the bottom of the Order Form.
By FAX: Copy the Order Form and send it on our FAX line: **1-800-224-6699 or 520-544-3086.**

ORDER FORM

HOME PLANNERS, LLC, wholly owned by Hanley-Wood, LLC
3275 WEST INA ROAD, SUITE 110
TUCSON, ARIZONA 85741

THE BASIC BLUEPRINT PACKAGE
Rush me the following (please refer to the Plans Index and Price Schedule on page 158):
___ Set(s) of Blueprints for Plan Number(s)_____. $_____
___ Set(s) of Reproducible Vellum(s)_____. $_____
___ Additional Identical Blueprints in same order @$60 per set $_____
___ Surcharge for Reverse Blueprints @$25 per set $_____

ADDITIONAL PRODUCTS
Rush me the following:
___ 24"x36" Black & White Rendering
    for Plan Number(s) _____ $_____
___ Specification Outlines @$10 each. $_____
___ Detail Sets @ $14.95 each; any two for $22.95; any three for $29.95; all four for $39.95 (save $19.85.) $_____
    ___Plumbing___Electrical___Construction___Mechanical
    (These helpful details provide general construction advice and are not specific to any single plan.)

POSTAGE AND HANDLING
DELIVERY (No CODs, Requires street address—No P.O. Boxes)
• Regular service (Allow 7-10 business days delivery) $15
• Priority (Allow 4-5 business days delivery) $25
• Express (Allow 3 business days delivery) $40

POSTAGE (From box above) $_____
SUBTOTAL $_____
SALES TAX (AZ, MI & WA residents please add
                appropriate state & local sales tax.) $_____
TOTAL (Subtotal and Tax) $_____

YOUR ADDRESS (please print)
Name _____
Street _____
City _____ State _____ Zip _____
Daytime telephone number

(___) _____

FOR CREDIT CARD ORDERS ONLY
Please fill in the information below:
Credit card number _____
Exp. Date: Month/Year _____
Check one
  ❑ Visa   ❑ MasterCard   ❑ Discover Card   ❑ American Express

Signature _____
Please check appropriate box: ❑ Licensed Builder-Contractor
                                ❑ Homeowner

BLUEPRINTS MAY NOT BE EXCHANGED, RETURNED OR REFUNDED

ORDER TOLL FREE!
1-800-521-6797
or 520-297-8200

Order Form Key

TB45

Architectural Notes

If you have built castles in the air, your work need not be lost; there is where they should be. Now put foundations under them.

Henry David Thoreau